hor

ARTISAN *New York*

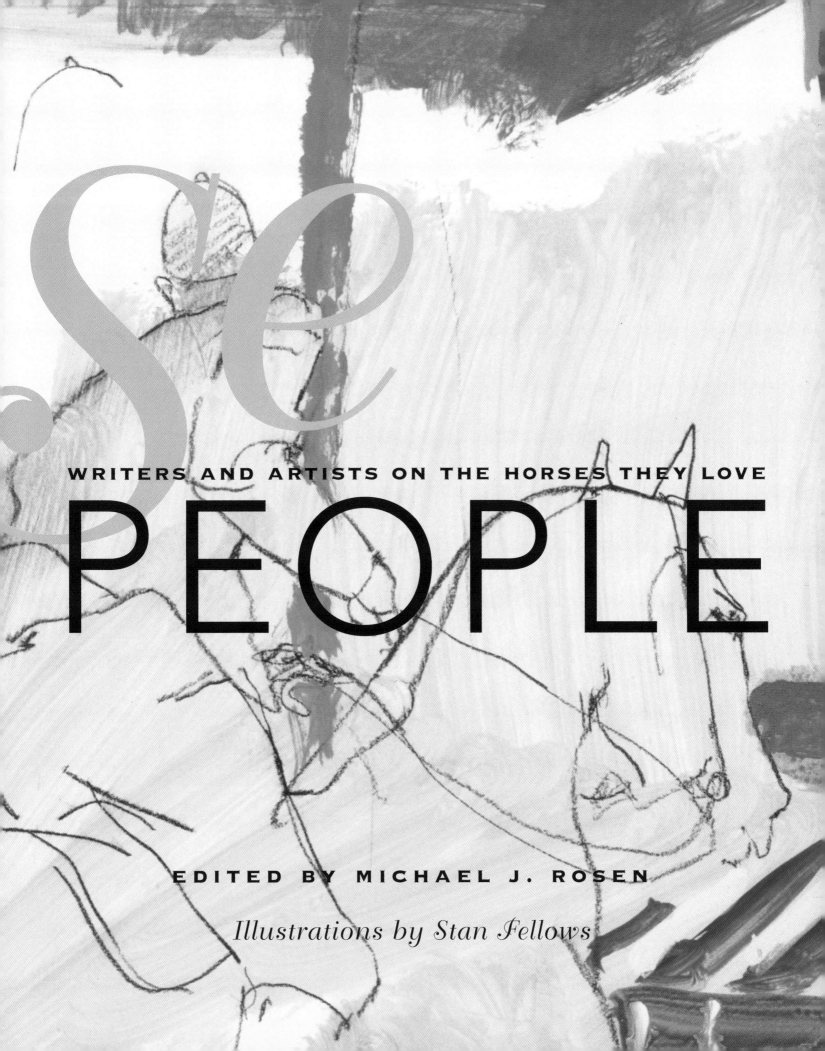

Horse

WRITERS AND ARTISTS ON THE HORSES THEY LOVE

PEOPLE

EDITED BY MICHAEL J. ROSEN

Illustrations by Stan Fellows

Compilations and Introduction copyright © Michael J. Rosen
Page 160 constitutes an extension of this copyright page.

Editor: Laurie Orseck
Designer: Alexandra Maldonado
Production Director: Hope Koturo

Library of Congress Cataloging-in-Publication Data
Horse People : writers and artists on their love of horses / [compiled by]
Michael J. Rosen : illustrations by Stan Fellows.
p.   cm..
isbn 1–885183–93–3
1. Horses--United States--Anecdotes.   2. Horses--United States--Pictorial works.
3. Horses in art.   4. Authors, American--Anecdotes.   5. Artists--United States--Anecdotes.
6. Horsemen and horsewomen--United States--Anecdotes.   I. Rosen, Michael J., 1954–
SF301.H67   1998
700'.46296655--dc2   97–45059
cip
ISBN 1–57965–212–3 (paper)
First published in 1998 by Artisan
A division of Workman Publishing Company, Inc.
708 Broadway, New York, New York 10003-9555
www.artisanbooks.com
Printed in China
10 9 8 7 6 5 4 3 2 1
First paperback edition, 2002

Photograph page 1 by Sue Kyllönen; pages 2-3 by Michael Paraskevas;
page 5 by Robb Kendrick; pages 6-7 by Michael Houghton

Contents

introduction

A SENSE OF HORSES

When I was younger, the whole of summer hinged on those few hours each week at the camp stable, just as the whole of the school year merely anticipated summer vacation.

I devoted myself to horseback riding. That, and swimming. Team competition left me anxious on the sidelines, but at the stables, the horse and I faced greater opponents: We outmaneuvered gravity, vanquished separate fears, and attempted a mediating language of touch and balance, where words were hardly uttered.

Did I love riding because I was good? Was I good because I loved it? I'd climb in the saddle, and gradually, other riders, other horses in the ring, whatever it was I didn't want to do after camp or beginning junior high—it all ceased to exist, along with the rest of my life on the ground, shrinking, fading behind our dusty trail.

That last summer of camp, Sparky was my own horse. It never dawned on me that each morning she was some other camper's, since I rode in the afternoon. I chose her from my instructor Ricki's description of Sparky's ideal rider: self-assured, consistent, with enough authority so the horse wouldn't take control. I wanted that challenge. Maybe I just wanted a beautiful horse with what Ricki called "a flea-bitten gray" coat. Or maybe it was Sparky's eyes: blue, like a sapphire, that made stars of sunlight.

Each session, we'd saddle up, practice maneuvers, and then parade out of the ring and across a plank bridge that, like a colossal xylophone, echoed the horses' hooves as they struck each board. We'd trail-ride in the forest for twenty minutes or so until we reached the meadow, where we'd have "open practice," meaning a chance to break loose. Though Ricki hadn't taught any gait faster than a canter, some horses, Sparky included, had to gallop. Suddenly the *one, two* and *three, four* of her hooves vanished into a liftoff, a levitation I felt the way you can feel the instant a plane lifts off or a roller coaster dips, and I'd be weightless, hardly resting in the saddle, my heart clop-clopping its own rapid gait as I hovered at a velocity only the tears that the wind jerked from my eyes revealed. In those moments—no more than a minute or two—the earth vanished entirely beneath us: She had become Pegasus, the winged Greek horse, and by some miracle, a twelve-year-old mortal had been chosen to ride her.

Sparky performed as no other horse I'd ridden. Each session, I sensed improvement. I settled into her trot. Reined more clearly. The moment I signaled to canter, she responded. Before Sparky, I'd never appreciated what Ricki meant about how horse and rider work toward a harmony that merges powers and thoughts.

One day, Gibby the stable owner's son replaced Ricki. She'd been injured, he explained. A horse had kicked her, crushed four ribs. "See, even experts can't be too careful." Though we vaguely knew Gibby, he didn't know us. For two solid weeks, he had us circle him in the corral while he pelted dirt clods at horses that weren't minding.

Someone besides us kids must have complained. For his final session, Gibby walked us to the meadow. "You're on your own," he said, "just don't run 'em." Then he dismounted and gathered up dirt clods.

"I said, don't race her," Gibby shouted at someone, just as I leaned into a canter.

A moment later, something whizzed past my chest. "You, for crying out loud! Listen!"

I jerked Sparky to a halt. "Me? You want me?"

"Yes, you! Too many holes to be running a blind animal! Trot her. Got it?"

"What? Sparky's not blind."

"Right. She's not blind, and you're not stupid." Then Gibby turned to yell at another camper.

I jumped down and stood in front of Sparky. Her eyes gazed, blinked, wondering no doubt why we weren't flying, why I was on the ground. I stared into her left eye, at the reflected clouds that were as much within her eye as in the sky. I stared at her other eye, at the receding herd of tiny horses and riders. I pressed my face to her muzzle and held my breath trying not to cry, then trying to stop.

Before long my counselor returned. No, I wasn't hurt. No, nothing happened. No, I don't care if the other kids see me crying. Ultimately, I said that I hated him . . . Gibby . . . camp . . . and everything else in a world that was this unfair. I wanted to stand in that field of rabbit warrens and groundhog burrows and tractor-wheel ditches and cry at least until camp ended, and maybe until summer ended, and quite possibly until I turned thirteen or thirty and this sadness, this overwhelmingly sorry

feeling—for Sparky, for myself?—had run dry with the tears.

But it didn't take that long. The bus was waiting. I took Sparky's reins and led her across the field, retracing a path my own two feet had never touched.

Her chest bandaged, Ricki returned the last day of camp to present achievement awards. She handed me a yellow card with a blue ribbon: the camp's top honor, the Pegasus Award. "Just don't hug me," she said.

I never saw Sparky after that summer. But I continued to think of that moment in the meadow, standing, stunned, forced to admit that true and impossible knowledge. And while that twelve-year-old boy, and, no doubt, that mythic horse, are long gone, it's only now I can see—instead of the sun, the woods, or other riders—my own reflection in that horse's cloudy, uncomprehending, sparkling eye.

I offer this brief story to suggest that for all the contributors here, and perhaps for all horse people, this animal performs one other task beyond whatever we may ask of it. Beyond jumping, hauling, conveying, racing, or any other work, the horse teaches. Sometimes it's confidence; other times, humility. Or respect. Honesty. Fairness. A lesson in overcoming this penchant we have for impatience or in defeating fear—of falling, of failing, or even of loving something frail as a horse or any other creature. As David Romtvedt writes, of a friend whose horse is dying, "I looked at Jean and realized that these feelings were not some easy sentimentalization—loving an animal because it requires less than loving another person. Instead I saw that Jean's love of the horses—and mine, too—was a way to have union with another world."

In fact, a horse requires much more from us—more training, space, money, time, trust, respect, deference, work—and thereby taxes nothing less than the most genuine part of our nature. Our true character must rise to the challenge, admit failure, or be taught, and thereby changed.

One thing these writers' experiences with their horses has taught me is how overeager we are to assign a single emotion (and too much rationalization) to the intense experiences we have. Horses help us to sustain, rather than prematurely resolve, the matrix of giddiness and frustration, hope and senselessness, enthusiasm and arrogance, that directs or dazes us every hour. Horse people listen to horses, not only to train them as "horse whisperer" Monty Roberts does, but to hear, in the perfect acoustics of a horse's returned silence, the stuff and nonsense we tell ourselves.

Why else are these personal essays so moving? Why else would such renowned authors, known less for their passion for horses than their passion for language, have written at the pitch of revelation: exhilarated, baffled, rapturous, smitten voices that touch on nothing less than our place on earth. And while *Horse People* includes humorous and courageous stories similar to ones that might feature a dog or cat, most essays here approach the religious in their reverence, the legendary in their awe. To describe any sustained time with a horse is to undertake self-reflection. An Arabic proverb compounds the reasons: "When a man rides his horse he forgets about God, and when he dismounts he forgets about his horse." Perhaps it is because no other animal in our lives perpetuates such dichotomies: enigmatic yet knowable, wild yet manageable, dangerous yet needful.

Even without wings or a unicorn's horn, the horse is our one extant mythical creature (as Eric Rohmann's illustration on page 155 suggests), whose physical prowess is second only to its power over our imagination. The horse brings us as close as we'll come to flying, though even our hubris can't get us aloft. The horse provided humankind's first vehicle for time travel and for space travel, and still brings worlds beyond our reach and gaze. The horse was our ancestors' wealth, authority, transport, rank, weapon, and machine, and still has not outlived such usefulness.

What other creature so preoccupies us in our youth? When no real horse fulfilled Candyce Barnes's girlhood wish each Christmas, she "created Phantom, who lived in my room, accompanied me everywhere, and ate off my plate during dinner (like me, Phantom hated chicken potpie and English peas)."

What other animal summons memory with such ache? As Jane Smiley writes: "After twenty years I resumed horseback riding. The moment was Proustian—I walked into a stable, and smelled the sweet, sour, green, moist richness of muck and it filled me with longing."

Of what besides horseback riding could Diane Ackerman say: "For those slender moments, I felt heart-poundingly creatural, and reveled in the thrill of speed and sunlight, part of an earth-ecstacy as old as the runes." Or could Gary Gildner say, remembering his first ride as a boy: ". . . there was a better perch from which to view eternity—or, at least the thing that seems will go on forever—even though we only went slowly around and around and eventually stopped."

Of what besides years of partnering with a horse could Tess Gallagher write, "Our two hearts were skywriters for a time against and above the earth. With her I had hoofbeats like muffled breaths pressed into the ground."

These are not writers given to flights of fancy and new-age thralldom. These are simply horse people, one after another, grappling with words for experiences that exceed us, relationships that throw our overwrought mechanism of speech out of gear, leaving us in the shared silence that the horse, and the rest of nature, provides.

Combined with images by contemporary artists and photographers who have fixed their attention on the horse and its grand, diminishing place in our world, *Horse People* pays homage to "one of the world's most alluring mysteries," to quote Michelle Huneven. Tributes, confessions, celebrations, elegies, monologues, and, indeed, stories—each speaks of the horse and its nature, but also of us horse people, an equally gregarious, skittish, breakable, earthbound species, riding these same populous plains, beneath this same unknowable heaven.

—*Michael J. Rosen*

aStride the twilight

DIANE ACKERMAN

I love the disciplined panic of a horse flirting with a tantrum at every turn, the delicate, voluptuous play of muscles, the grace-sprung power. This became especially clear to me one cold winter day a few years ago, when I rode an Appaloosa mare bareback, trotting her swiftly through tight hairpin turns, and for the first time I really stuck without sliding or jiggling. My legs hugged her belly like a cinch, and her heart pounded against my knees as she paced. Deeply I sat, fixed to the slap, slap, slap, slap of her trot, and the counterpoint thud-plod, thud-plod of her heart, enchanted by a soft percussion I felt part of, floating above the syncopated rhythm like a melody. A sweet, leathery steam rose from her chest and neck. When I fretted her belly lightly with my calf, she rolled into a long rippling, and I felt at home in the pumping of her shoulders, the sweet dank odor of hot fur, the rhythmic gesturing of her head. My legs tingled with half a dozen pulses, some of them my own.

Reckless with exhilaration, I jumped her bareback over several low fences, gripping her steamy hide as we sprang over fence after fence, leaving earth for a moment between the blunt stanchions and leaping through the gristly winter light for the sun, setting right at the end of the valley like a hot yellow liquid pouring out. As my legs began to gently reason with her body, we rose over a fence like a fog bank, below which lay the world of humans. For those slender moments, I felt heart-poundingly creatural, and reveled in the thrill of speed and sunlight, part of an earth ecstasy as old as the runes. Life blew through my veins as the wind charged through the winter trees. Huge oily-looking ravens sounded as if they were choking on lengths of blanket. And then night began seeping over the hillsides like a long spill of black ink, erasing everything civilized and safe.

my grandfather and his belgians

GARY GILDNER

This is really about two horses, bourbon-colored Belgians, great big steppers that could strut beside a row of beans precise as ballet dancers, trailing a flock of white birds. But to tell about them properly I first have to say a little about my maternal grandfather.

His name was Stefan Szostak, a Pole. He left the Old Country as a teenager and arrived in Detroit just before the twentieth century. In 1902 he married a Polish-American girl from Hamtramck, my grandmother Aniela, whom he called Nelly. He said poems to her, poems by the heroic Adam Mickiewicz. And told her

such tales! How could my grandmother ever forget Queen Wanda of Kraków who, pursued by a German prince, leaped from her castle window into the deep waters of the Vistula, calling out with her last breath that she would rather marry a Polish river!

When they went walking Sunday afternoons in Detroit, keeping away from the traffic of cyclists and especially away from those powerful new machines that came along more and more now and made such a noise and threw oil on the driver—and on anyone else who got too close—and worst of all, from Aniela's point of view, spurted red flames, Stefan would wrap her in an arm and raise his fist, saying that the great and beautiful way to travel was by *kon!* By horse!

She was sixteen. He was a blacksmith, trained to shoe the animal he loved, but instead he found work in Henry Ford's foundry, tending the fires. One day he got splashed by molten steel. The scars on his cheek, neck, and back, years later when I saw them, were like flowers, pink peonies pressed to his skin.

In 1927, the fabulous year that Charles Augustus ("Lucky") Lindbergh soloed the Atlantic, Babe Ruth hit sixty home runs, and the stock market was soaring, my grandfather, who had saved some money, looked to the heavens as well. He retired, took his family out of Detroit, and became a gentleman farmer. Which my mother said was his dream. And the northern Michigan farm he bought, a rolling, mainly wooded place with a good stream moving through, was perfect for a dream—far better to look at and breathe in richly than to work. But when the market crashed two years later, he had to work it. Hard.

He was still working it when, at the close of World War II, I began spending my summers there. Three summers, anyway—my romantic education. I was a city kid, eight, nine, and ten, up from automotive Flint, and everything I remember about that time seems tethered to Prince and Nelly—even the rosy lump I wondered about on the neck of the old farmer kneeling bent and nut-wrinkled in the front pew of my grandparents' village church: an *egg,* Grandma whispered (not wanting, I'm sure, to get into goiters during Mass), and I believed her, remembering the raw potato Grandpa carried in his pocket to help loosen

his stiff leg as, draped in reins, he walked behind those full-rumped Belgians, crooning to them.

When he took them down to the creek for a drink, I too went down. But first—

I remember the woolly itch on the back of my neck from the scapular Grandma gave me, the Holy Family patch at one end, the Bleeding Heart at the other, one of them dangling past my belt and getting in the way when I had to pee fast, my shoulders and back prickly with hay and sweat. I remember running plenty ahead of Grandpa and Prince and Nelly and the hay cutter, my shins red and sore from kicking the cut stems, following beside the unmowed edge with my burlap bag flying—jumping over mice and garter snakes all snipped up in the cutter's wake, jumping over the sudden bright scatterings of newborn rabbits I failed to catch and run with to the bee-stippled orchard, among the windfallen Goldens, the spongy snows, and release; can remember and now almost touch the cold sweaty Mason jar of springwater waiting in the shade under a tree, can see myself wanting to lift it with both hands to my mouth, like him, the drops of water sparkling in his mustache, and wishing I too had a mustache I could wipe with the back of my wrist.

Now I see him pulling off the salt-slick harnesses and slapping the horses' withers and flanks, letting his hand—that big-knuckled hand from an old Brownie snapshot—linger on their foamy hindquarters; and now I can smell them, the sharp, sweet, barny odor of punky wood, old shoes, straw, and my own skin after running, waiting, and now I am cantering beside them down to the creek, into the creek, the wide hole where trout flash, the fine hairs on my face flat on the water, like Prince's, like Nelly's, like his, collecting bubbles, our muzzles in deep at last for a long, long drink.

Then my grandfather stood. Up to his hips in current, he pulled off his shirt and bathed those flowery shapes on his shoulders and back, shaking his head, a wild man slapping his sides, snorting; and when he was through, he hung one arm over Prince and one over Nelly who, up to their own hips, had been waiting for him to do just that. Although he was in his sixties, near the end of his life, to me my grandfather, exactly like those two companions, was of no age, a force, a collection of motion and silences and sudden bursts of sound that, were I smart enough then, I would have known was music.

Once, seeing me watching him on the hay wagon, he stopped the team and waved me over. He pulled me up, sat me between his legs, and gave me the reins to hold. Then he clicked his tongue to move Prince and Nelly along—along faster! Calling *Gee!* and *Haw!* until Grandma came rushing out to the field, her fist, her skirts, and the Polish flying, afraid I would be hurt . . . and he, his hands over mine, helped me steer the wagon around and around her, heightening her color further; and all the while a fine gold shower of hay dust falling, and he singing those sounds of recklessness and affection, that operatic dip and rise of murmur and huzzah, to her, to me, to the magnificent team (look at them! his proud arm proclaimed), and all of which I can still hear when I am happy.

Nights after chores, the honeyed glow from the kerosene lamp on the kitchen table softening his scars, he began to disappear. He did this so quietly and smoothly I could not believe he would return in the morning. Night after night in that honeyed light he ate his soup and bread, he knelt on the floor hunched over his rosary like a small bear come from the woods, and from farther and farther away in his throat came the sound of recklessness and huzzah ground down to a groan of satisfaction, as when he pressed his pink cheek into Nelly's or Prince's velvety lips, as when he lifted the shot of whiskey he allowed himself at day's close. Then he threw back the shot. Then from inside his shirt, where at first I thought he himself would crawl, he brought forth a book and was gone.

The summer I stayed in Flint to start baseball, Grandma found him beside the barn, among the hollyhocks, beyond which, a few feet, Prince and Nelly stood in their stalls. I turned eleven that August, and on my birthday, in a satin box, he lay with pennies on his eyes, his trimmed mustache nothing like the shaggy one flecked with hay dust that I knew, his pink patches, his face, white and shiny as a bowl. Hot all over, I slipped away to the creek and took off my blue wool suit, and drank, and shook my head like a wild man, like a horse, and saw falling on the water little more than my skinny shadow.

I did not know for a long time that Joseph Conrad was my grandfather's favorite writer. Nor that just before Mr. Savage the undertaker closed the coffin, Grandma put in there the last book he was reading, the one she had found him with beside the barn. I did not see her do this. Years later, on my way to Marquette to start my first teaching job, Grandma told me, reminded of it, she said, by all the books in my car. I wanted very much to know the name of that book. She couldn't tell me. Only that it was by "this Korzeniowski again, always Korzeniowski," she said.

Over drinks at a poetry festival, where I was to introduce him, I was telling Czeslaw Milosz about my grandfather. "I think that last book was *Heart of Darkness*." He raised his bushy eyebrows, raised his glass. Was there a better title to take into eternity?

Or was there a better, richer perch from which to view eternity than the granary roof, straddling its ridge, pretending this was my mount and the oats under my legs pure gold—seeing all around me the worlds I might visit, the barn with its high haymow, the creek, the orchard, all good places in which to leap, bathe, swing from limbs—and seeing my grandfather come across the yard like a man learning to walk, searching his way? Suddenly among the pecking chickens he thrust out his arms, as if he were showing them how an acrobat performed on a wire. At the granary he stopped; looking up he seemed puzzled; then he smiled, waved, and went on to the barn. When he came out he was leading Nelly, bringing her over to me. I understood, thrillingly, that I was to get down from the roof and onto the back of something far better. It was the first time he had made this offer. I sat on Nelly's broad brown powerful back, holding her bristly mane, smelling that warm-woodsy-wet-oats skin, and yes, there *was* a better perch from which to view eternity—or at least the thing that it seems will go on forever—even though we only went slowly around and around and eventually stopped.

At no time during those three summers—nor at Thanksgiving or Christmas or any other family gathering—did my grandfather and I ever exchange a word. He spoke Polish; I did not. He patted my head, he gave me a hand up, he helped me steer, he waved. He worked a farm he had not intended to work so hard, and he read a complex writer who tried, above everything, to be clear, to make us see. He had two horses. When plowing his fields he trailed a flock of white birds that he seemed to have conjured out of the soil; when he milked, pulling those freckled teats, bubbled hearts of sweet clover rose in his pail. When he sat in the orchard looking at the sky, I would climb a limb and watch, and wonder what held him so still. I do not know what he thought, really, except that in naming his horses he left a pretty good clue. When my grandmother told me he had once held her close and shouted that the great and beautiful way to travel was by horse, I saw him traveling by two, and shaking his head like a man who couldn't quite believe his luck.

bootS, saddle, to horSe, and Away!

CANDYCE BARNES

I've had horses all my life—some were fictional horses or equine film stars, a few were wooden or plastic, one was imaginary, and several were real. If you'd asked me when I was two or three, my favorite would no doubt have been my red and black Wonder horse suspended from his stand by coiled springs. I rode that horse so long and hard my Uncle Tommy had to shore it up with springs that looked like they'd come off a railroad freight car.

By the time I was five and going to the grocery store on weekly shopping expeditions with my mother and grandmother, my love transferred to a fiberglass palomino stallion on some sort of mechanical base out in front of the Jitney Jungle. It had what looked like the nickel-plated handle of a baseball bat where the saddle horn should have been—a technological breakthrough for the modern horseman: speed control. Push a nickel into the plunger and bucket along at the pace of your choice next to huge humpback ridges of Black Diamond and Jubilee watermelons. Yeah, I used to ride out of the Black Diamond spread (pause to spit), had me a little ol' palomino stallion named Jubilee . . .

Horse crazy. It happens to a lot of little girls. I think my case was fairly modest considering the more virulent strains of the epizootic. When I watched cowboy movies (and God knows I am still a sucker for a Republic Western), it was the horses that held me in thrall. And while I had holsters and guns aplenty, my interest wasn't the gunfight at the OK Corral, but riding off into the sunset on Topper, or Champion, or Trigger. Tarzan, Diablo, or Silver.

Probably the first real horse I ever rode was at the Memphis Zoo: a sort of living merry-go-round of nasty-tempered Shetland ponies attached by poles to a wheel. Very tame for someone who'd ridden a wild palomino stallion. Eventually, the zoo built a little track where the ponies were loose—of course, you had to ride them around a small ring, within a fenced corridor almost too narrow for the ponies to pass side by side. The reins were tied to the saddle and an attendant adjusted your stirrups, but you were free to kick your pony (all of whom were shaped like oil drums) if your legs were long enough. I figured even Gene Autry had to start somewhere.

Every Christmas, my wish was the same: a horse. When no real horse ever appeared under the tree, I created Phantom, who lived in my room, accompanied me everywhere, and ate off my plate during dinner (like me, Phantom hated chicken potpie and English peas—a fact not lost on my mother). I begged for a horse in increments. Just a saddle to start with, I said. I'd cinch it to the doghouse. Well, hey, Steve Cauthen practiced on hay bales.

I read every horse book ever written. I am sure this is not an exaggeration. Ask the beleaguered librarians at the Highland Branch of the Cossett Library in Memphis, Tennessee. These borrowings were supplemented by my Aunt Rudy, who provided me with a constant stream of Black Stallion books. I read and reread equine classics: *Black Beauty, My Friend Flicka, Misty of Chincoteague.* I read anything that had a horse on it or in it.

The Strawberry Roan, That Dodger Horse, Spin and Marty.

I had horse figurines, horse wallpaper, horse friends. Curtains printed with hunter-jumpers lifting over double oxers; a bedspread that revealed the more tranquil, domestic side of the horse family: antic foals drinking at the pond; mares gossiping at the fence. Forced by the Memphis Board of Education to go to school instead of to a ranch, I played "horsey" with similarly inclined chums at every recess, when I became a wild mustang. To this day I fight the urge to nicker when I see carrots.

I was about ten when my best friend got a real mare named Minnie Pearl; I was allowed to go to the Whitehaven Saddle Club with Margie Lane and ride Minnie. As I recall, Minnie was a fairly nondescript black saddle horse who carried her neck low and always looked like she was sniffing for the trail. She had a prickly temper with other horses, and battle scars that made it look as though she'd been gnawed on by rats, but we saw her as a queen among horses.

The trip out to catch Minnie, across the pasture with a bucket of sweet feed, was the grandest adventure of all: the sweet feed we scooped out of a dusty bin in a tack room that smelled of leather and saddle soap. It made a sort of tinny hissing as it poured into the bucket. In my memory, it's always winter, the late-afternoon light pale as oats. We'd lift the latch on the pasture gate and walk through dry, red sage grass on down a little gully and up towards the stand of pin oaks where the clay was a strange persimmon color. Here Minnie loved to wallow and rub her back.

Soon it would begin: a slow wraithlike materialization of horses. Roans, chestnuts, bays, blacks, pintos, buckskins. Silent at first, then occasional whinnies—like heraldic trumpets. Drawn by the sweet feed. We'd be surrounded by gently snorting horses, shuffling towards us like patients in a hospital ward. Sometimes they'd play at being spooked and shy away if you tried to pat them, but usually they just came forward and bumped you with their muzzles. There we'd be, surrounded, lightly buffeted by these nearly mystical creatures—the soft whoosh of their breath, the smell of horse, the friendliness of it all. A very collegial feeling.

When you are of a certain age (say, around twelve or thirteen), and of a certain disposition (somewhat irrationally attracted to horses), there is no look quite as charming as wellies, jeans, and horse snot across the front of your sweater. There is no perfume more alluring than Eau de Riding Stable. Horses, manure, hay, leather, sweet feed, saddle soap—it has quite a "nose." It fires the imagination and fevers the brain. There is something about picking a hoof or mucking out a stall that imprints you with horses forevermore.

I had become an addict. Family vacations had to be charted to places like Gulf Hills Dude Ranch. There are pictures of me grinning insanely on top of a big hammerheaded pinto named Buster who had a walleye and a gait like he'd been smoking pot. Even the infamous Breakfast Ride at Lake Tanneycomo, where my horse seemed to be drawn at high speed to any blade of grass that grew at the edge of a precipice, could not dissuade me—I had to have my own horse. There were riding stables with a litany of horses who were "mine": Frosty, Traveller, Buck, Rebel, Sunny, Gunner, Little Chief. And finally there was Major.

My parents gave in when I was twelve—it had been

a long campaign. Mister Major. Named after my Aunt Major, who, as family lore recounted, had gone riding with her beau (soon to be Uncle Hunter). When her horse bolted, Aunt Major screamed in genteel Victorian fashion: "*Whoa* your horse and *whoa* mine, too!"

Major was a failed Standardbred racehorse. Seventeen and one half hands high. Copper-colored, with a flaxen mane and tail. His name until I got him had been Shine. And now he was all mine. For the next six years I lived and breathed with but one purpose: to ride Major. During the week, my mother carted me out in the afternoons; on weekends, she'd drop me at dawn and return at dark. If I had not gone to college, I would doubtless have gone through the reverse of the tadpole's evolutionary progress and lost my legs. I no longer needed them. I could easily eat and come close to sleeping on the back of Major. My first kiss started on his back (we later retired to some pine straw, chaperoned by his discreet presence).

Even though I no longer have a horse, I still count myself a horseman. Fortunately, I have friends with horses. And there's nothing I relish quite so much as going to the stables, hanging out, absorbing the smells, feeding an apple or two, and doing an Eskimo nose rub with a friendly horse. Is there anything finer, more delicate, and wonderful than a horse's muzzle?

Christmas is not all that far off, and my mother is nudging me about a wish list. When you are of a certain age (say, around forty-seven or forty-eight) and of a certain disposition (say, not yet grown-up), there's always one special thing to wish for. Just a saddle to start with, I think.

horsey girl

I was a "horsey girl." It started with my first pony ride, grew to drawings covering all my notebooks, and settled into riding every afternoon and weekend. I was hooked from the first nicker, the first flowing mane and soft muzzle. The realization that at an age when decisions were usually made by others, I could experience freedom and control from the back of a twelve-hundred-pound animal confirmed my "horsey girl" status. Even when classmates moved their seats away from me in response to the manure clinging to my shoes, I thought it would last forever.

Somewhere after Lytle Nell and Canadian Blue, after Pony Club and high school, I stopped riding. My time was spent with art school, then career goals. Eighteen years later I found myself at a riding academy, scouting a site to shoot my next video. Within half an hour I was astride a chestnut gelding, taking a lesson.

I now spend most mornings at the barn and consider it an extension of my studio. I still don't know if that first video piece was a natural progression in my artistic exploration of female identity, or just a need to get back in the saddle. Whichever, the following images are of video installations by a "horsey girl."

Celeste in her bedroom (C-print)

Girls and Horses (video projections)

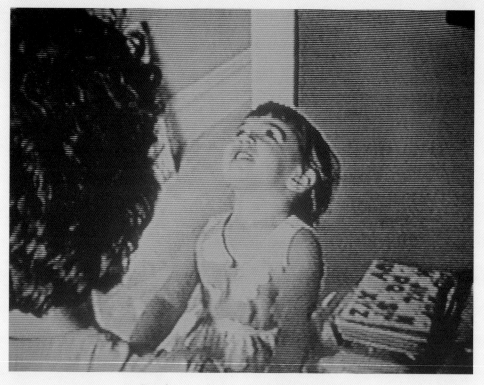

Caroline and Karen playing horsey

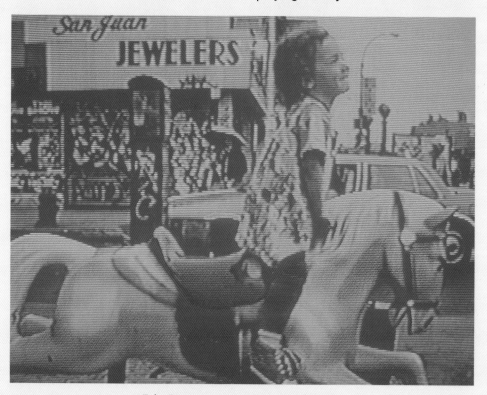

Eda Faye on coin-operated horse

Jacqui and Marc playing horsey

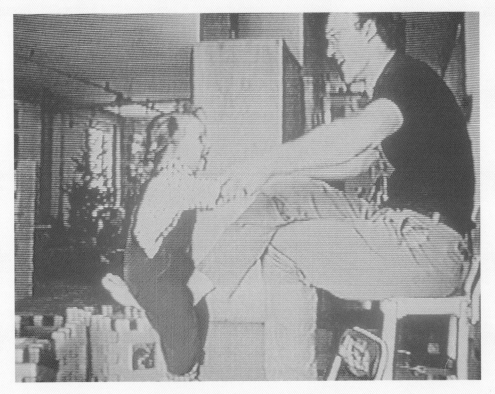

Molly and Andrew playing horsey

horSe riffs (a journal)

MEREDITH MONK

Dream Girl, Laddie, Amber, Splash. I am six, alone, at camp. Watching the horses go around and around the ring, my friend Lana and I stand transfixed. The pungent smell, the sand flying around from the hooves, the rhythmic sound like my heartbeat, like my blood. I start drawing horses, horses of every color, with pink and blue stripes, with green spots. Horses stretched out and flattened into an impossible angle with eyes larger than their heads.

Pink Lady, Miss Boots, Trader. I am eight. In my bedroom are two portraits of horses. One chestnut, one black. I wake up in the morning talking to them, I go to sleep singing to them. Sometimes, when I look at them, they turn into different things: a mountain, a monster, a person. I have learned to ride with Chris and then Mr. Davies and then the Bardens. I am so small that the stirrup leathers have to be rolled around and around the buckle. I am like a little mosquito on those gigantic backs and just as mean. I pull the horses around to get them to do what I want. My teacher laughs.

In a dream forty years later, a black mare says to me over and over, "Take courage. Take courage." Her nose is so soft and kind that I sob and sob. I can't believe that anything can be as soft; like black velvet, like a newborn peach. A few months later, I begin riding again.

Jazzman, Mac, Bubba, Cedric, J. J., Brownie . . . Brownie, my friend and companion. You clever pony, as brown and rich as your name. Yes, you are on the horse/pony border: too big and proud to be a pony, too clever and devilish to be a horse. Flying over jumps, flying high, flying wide, sometimes my eyes open, sometimes my eyes closed. But you, jumping with all your heart, your heart huge, expanding wider and wider, dauntless, relentless in your courage. I have laughed with you when you start galloping in the middle of the field without a warning because you have heard, you have smelled, you have seen, way up on the hill, as small as ants (to *my* eyes), your friends the geldings playing a game of tag.

I wonder where it comes from, this love of horses. Quincy, Arizona, Hot Shot, Bill. I am in Poland singing my songs. I am fifty-three. I want to visit Lomza and Stavisky, the places I have heard about, the first homes of Grandpa and Grandma. No one in the family knows very much about the past in the old country. No one has asked questions. How I wish I had been old enough to know better, to ask and ask. I remember the sweetness of Grandpa, taking me to the candy store, holding my hand. I remember Grandma in her tiny garden pulling weeds, her arms, brown and strong, flowing from the puffed sleeves of her embroidered peasant blouse; in her kitchen making *teglach*, honey cake, overcooked chicken; in her bedroom unraveling her long, long white braids that during the day she had wound around her head.

After my concerts in Warsaw, the sponsor arranges a car to take me to Lomza, my grandfather's hometown. I hear my father telling me how Grandpa used to tease Grandma, "Libby, my darling, you're just a country hick, but I come from the big town of Lomza!" As we come to it, I realize that, yes, it *is* too big a town to find out anything about my family in one afternoon. I ask the driver to please continue to the village of Stavisky.

In Stavisky there are no Jews left, yet the old wooden houses of the Jewish streets remain, still inhabited by people who stare from the shuttered windows. News of our arrival travels fast, especially since a crew from Polish TV is filming my visit. The oldest man in the village remembers my grandmother because it was unusual for a woman, particularly a Jewish woman, to drive a horse and wagon. One of the few stories that my father knew about the old country was that Grandma transported Jews in her wagon, hidden under hay, to the border, where they continued on alone to the port, to the boat, to America.

The film crew has a surprise for me: They have borrowed a draft horse and wagon from a farmer so that I can drive it just as my grandmother did so many years ago. As I yell *haaaa!* or *prrrrr!* the horse goes and stops and the farmer, walking ahead of me, leads me to where he thinks my grandmother's family lived: on the corner of Ulica Furmanska, "Horse Wagon Driver Street."

❧

Horse shows, drill teams, red horses, spotted horses, golden horses. Galloping along the beach in California, up and down grassy hills in Maine, riding in England, in Germany, in Brazil, in Nepal. Falling in the woods, falling in the ring, falling, falling, getting back up shaken but wanting to go on. The mystery continues like a heartbeat, like my blood.

MICHAEL PARASKEVAS

jumping

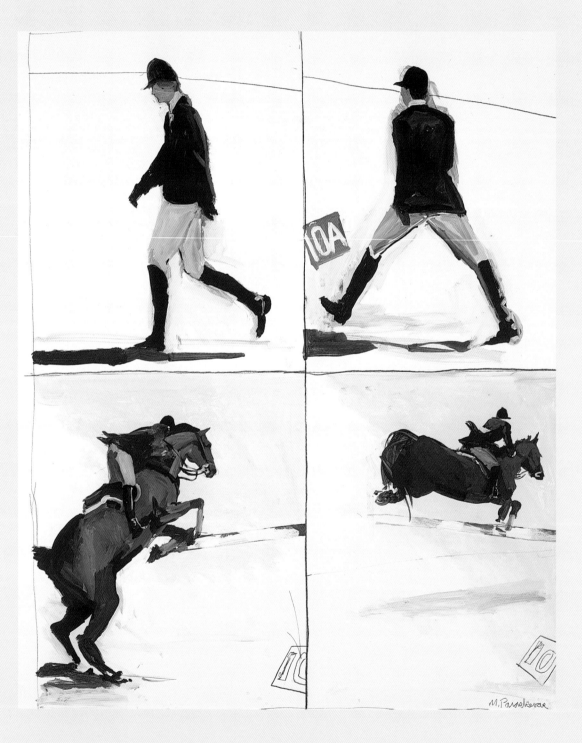

nOthing but troUble since the day he was bOrn

JANA HARRIS

There is no other way to describe Byron. Everything about him was wrong. When he was unloaded from the horse van on a cloudy October Monday, he was the ugliest weanling I'd ever seen. The color of wet cement, scrawny, hammerheaded, with marble frog eyes too narrowly spaced. No wonder his dam kicked him in the head. There had been a wild ice gale the night before, so violent that falling trees had killed several pigeons roosting in the haymow. Recalling the terrible cracking noise the Alaska blue spruce near the barn made as it split apart, I imagined that that might have been the sound of Byron's jawbones breaking.

Byron had been sent to my farm in the foothills of the Cascade Mountains from a Thoroughbred breeder near the Canadian border to recover from his fracture and to be a pasture mate to my gray six-month-old foal, Colette. I'd had no other foals that year, and horses mature better mentally and physically if they have the opportunity to romp with youngsters their own age. In the jargon of the industry, this is called "laying down bone."

Byron? Wherever did he get that name, I wondered as I lead him to his box next to Colette's roomy double-size nursery stall. Colette had a sweet temper, a lovely dish face, and enormous soulful walnut eyes. She put her head over the stall door, sniffed noses with Byron, then pinned her ears, turning her butt to the door. In equine body language, this maneuver read: Go home, ugly.

Horses have a keen sense of smell, and I chalked Colette's adverse reaction to her new best friend as her sensory ability to ferret out the odor of surgery that lingered on Byron's recently wired-together lower and upper mandibles.

An hour later, while on the phone to the barn manager at Magic Meadow Race Stable getting Byron's feed and medication instructions, I asked how he got his name. Default, the manager told me. When Philipa's Magic took offense at the gray colt's familiarity with her new foal, Philipa's Pride, and whacked him in the head, the grooms had started calling him Beaver-eater. When his mother divvied out the same punishment a day later, the name stuck. The Jockey Club, however, takes a dim view of sexually explicit expressions, so Beaver, etc., evolved into Byron's Song.

Static crackled on the telephone line, followed by a long pause wherein I should have asked, "And this is what you sent to me as a companion to my already sick foal?" Colette wasn't a Thoroughbred bound for the racetrack, she was a Warmblood, a sort of cross between a racehorse and a workhorse, bound for a riding discipline called dressage that has been likened to ballet on horseback. Her bones had grown more rapidly than her tendons and she was relegated to a special diet of low-protein hay and muscle relaxers.

I had hoped to house both foals in the large nursery stall, but within ten seconds of leading Byron into Colette's roomy indoor run, the hair started to fly. For the first time in her life, my little gray filly planted her hind hooves into the stall wall, knocking out several two-by-sixes. Byron was quickly removed and stalled two boxes away, which didn't seem to be far enough for Colette.

Turning the new pasture mates out together in a grassy paddock the following day met with a little less friction, at least for the first five minutes while the two were distracted by pigeon calls. The cries of birds for their lost mates even cut into the barn cat Yoda's heart.

Colette had a large round behind, a short back, and a neck attached at the top of her withers, effecting the posture of a sea horse. Half her size, Byron resembled something between a charred chicken bone and one of the fallen tree limbs that littered the back pasture. After the pigeons reorganized themselves on the barn roof, things seemed uneventful for the length of time it took Colette to pick a corner of the corral and position herself with her rear end aimed at the center of the turnout and one hind foot cocked. She resembled a loaded cannon. Byron danced around her, eager to light her fuse. Two steps forward, one step back, I thought, securing a lead rope to Byron's halter, then moving him into an adjacent paddock.

The other horses eyed the newcomer suspiciously. When none would even so much as play "touch nose" with him through the fence rails, Byron began to fly around his turnout like an electron. Between bites of grass the yearlings, Miss Piggy and Kermit, stared at him sidelong. Mom, Colette's dam, stared transfixed for several seconds, then galloped to the far corner of the pasture as if Byron were a space alien. Before fleeing, Mom turned so quickly that she pulled both front shoes off her hooves and they flew through the air as though she'd thrown them at the little gray colt. Not even the two older riding geldings could be induced into running the fence line. I watched Byron try to entice Willie Africa into a biting match between the lowest rail and the ground, imagining that the baby racehorse compared his saucer-size feet to Willie's dinner-platter hooves.

We spent the day cleaning up after the storm, collecting fallen limbs, repairing broken fence rails and downed gutters. During barn check that night, Byron's stall looked as if the hundred-mile-an-hour gusts of the day before had blasted through it. He'd torn his grain bucket off the wall, stepped on his salt block, defecated in his water bucket, and pawed a hole in the floor. His half-eaten hay rations had been trod upon. Watching Byron eat made me wince. What few milk teeth remained in his mouth hit in a nerve-jarring clap-clap sound. Though cracked corn and rolled oats dribbled out of his mouth, no expression of discomfort crossed his face. I'd give him one thing: He had the devil's willingness to thrive.

During morning feeding two days later, I noticed a lone pigeon roosting in the rafters of Byron's stall. He (with a ruff like that the bird had to be male) was there again that night. One of the birds that lost his spouse in the storm, I thought. Since pigeons in my neck of the woods mate for life, I felt a pang of sadness for the little gray bird that gleamed green in the early winter sun, then remembered that messy pigeons were hardly welcome guests. When Byron, who had by now earned the barn name Nothing But Trouble (shortened to Nothing But), lay down, Pij swooped out of the rafters and began eating the water-and-molasses-soaked grain that had fallen from the weanling's mouth.

Was it loneliness or Pij's fog-colored feathers and the foal's mousy coat that bound them? In the week following, Pij moved from the barn beams to the top plank of the stall divider, gliding down to peck the manger floor free of corn right alongside Byron as the weanling ate his dinner rations. During daytime turnout, the nurse mare continued to pin her ears at the newcomer, eyeing him as if he were a green fly. Colette kept as far away from his paddock fence as possible. Once, I carried Byron's noon hay rations to him in his turnout pen, and the weanling decided that I was someone to rear and run with. Never, before or since, have I come so close to getting kicked in the head by a horse. In his stall that night, however, Byron was sweetness and light as he and Pij ate grain together from the manger. I watched the foal gently butt the bird aside with his teacup-size muzzle, then stand protectively over Pij, shielding him from Yoda's lustful feline eyes.

The first morning of November was a day so clear that the glaciers on the side of White Horse Mountain glowed pink in the rising sun. Leading Byron to his paddock, I noticed that Pij followed, perching on a gatepost. Then—I could not believe my eyes—Pij flew the fence line as Byron galloped after him, up and back. Colette's head turned, her stunned stare mirroring mine. A pigeon exercising a race colt? As Pij circled overhead, Byron began running circuits around the rectangular-shaped corral. His spidery legs blurred as he galloped into the corner, across the diagonal, around the far turn, down the home stretch, faster, fast enough to out-fly a bird to the polelike water-bucket-of-a-finish-line near the gate.

After Thanksgiving, I began turning the weanling out in the wooded back pasture, and then the pond pasture. Each time the bird followed Byron from his stall. Always Pij began to fly around the fence line. Always Byron ignored the lush year-round grass and ran after the bird, ringing the racecourse that had been bred into his genes. And always foal trailed bird, finally overtaking the gray-green wingspan. On New Year's Day, according to Jockey Club rules, Byron officially became a yearling. His chest had broadened and the muscles in his upper forelegs had gained definition. The horn of his hooves grew straight and dark and strong. As horse and bird bolted into their morning workout, the flair of Byron's nostrils widened, turning the rose hue of a mountain sunrise.

By February, Byron's jaw had healed without scar or disfigurement, and it was almost certain that by the time he turned two he'd be able to tolerate a snaffle bit in his mouth and begin his first thirty days of training. On the Saturday after Valentine's Day, a sleek silver tractor-trailer pulled into my driveway. We loaded Byron onto the ten-horse van that would whisk him up the Interstate, across the border, and back to the farm in the Kootenai where he'd been born.

The day Byron left, Pij vanished. I never saw either of them again. I like to think of Byron's Song running the grassy turf of British Columbia racecourses, a lithe grindstone-colored gelding leading the field as he chases a ruff-necked bird eight furlongs across the finish line into history.

three storieS

DAVID ROMTVEDT

I.FAVORITE SONG

My brother-in-law George, my sister Laura, and their two kids, Maggie and Sy, are visiting from North Carolina. They've been here in Wyoming before and spent time with Margo and me and our daughter, Caitlin, at the ranch. But always in summer, when it's so hot and dry that your tongue feels like a week-old biscuit trapped in your mouth.

George is a nut for arrowhead hunting. And he loves horses so we go out riding, staring at the ground, hopping off every few yards to look at some bright flash in the clay and sand. I've got a picture of George riding our old bay Harold. George is waving. He's all gangly and happy. Harold's jerking his head down to see if there might be a tuft of grass he can pull up before it gets any bigger.

That's summer. Now it's winter. Two nights ago the thermometer nailed into a cottonwood tree by the creek read -42° F. And in town it was thirty below. George says he'd like to ride around the ranch now, just kind of feel what winter's like.

"It's a beautiful day," he says.

And it is. Full sun and the midday temperature has risen to about zero. I love this kind of weather and say, "Sure, let's go. Penelope's the only horse in, though— she's got arthritis and we keep her close in winter. Can't ride her. We'll have to walk to find the other horses. They're somewhere in the River Pasture."

Knowing that this pasture is around seven thousand acres, my sister Laura's dubious but agrees she'll go, too. Margo is forced to stay behind and baby-sit. If we find the horses, we'll bring them in and everybody can ride—kids, too.

"So," George says as we start walking. "You know that every horse's favorite song is 'Streets of Laredo'?"

"I didn't know that."

"Yeah, sure, watch." He walks to the barn and sings the song—"Da-daa-da-da, da-da; da-daa-da-da, da-da." Penelope lifts her head and George says, "See that? Proof."

But as we walk across the creek bed and up toward the Lizard Rocks, Laura says that actually horses prefer "I'm an Old Cowhand from the Rio Grande." Then she makes up a new line to the song, "I'm an old cowgirl from another world."

George looks at her funny and she says, "Wyoming, dontcha know, another world." Then she starts a snow-ball fight.

We walk on for two more hours and finally find the horses all winter-jumpy, so it takes a long time to get a rope on one of them. But we finally do and set off walking home, the other horses trailing the one we're leading. George's hard leather shoes are frozen so that when he takes a step there's a creaking noise, a haywire song in the crusted snow. This is a scary sound to winter-shy horses. With each creak, Nut Maggot (her real name is Cinnamon but she's got a foul temper) crow-hops to one side like she's going to fall off a cliff and Trouble jerks his head like God poked him with a sharp stick.

Unsure of exactly how deep the snowed-in ditches and draws are, we walk slowly, unsteadily. As we walk we make up the rest of Laura's song:

I'm an old cowgirl from another world.
When I wave my arms I fly
and I can smell you with my eyes.
On my horse I never ride though she's
always by my side.
Well, you may think I'm strange
but I understand the range.

Got a neoprene rope, polyurethane chaps,
stainless-steel boots and a fiberglass hat,
wear my Mylar gloves on my long hairy arms,
yippee ky yo ky yea, whoo,
yippee ky yo ky yea.

On Saturn's rings I learned to rope
down a planetary slope.
Caught a comet by the tail,
through the universe I sail.
Got no federal graze permit,
ain't got no federal government.
Escaped the bureaucratic mess
so no galactic neural stress.

Got a neoprene rope, polyurethane chaps,
stainless-steel boots and a fiberglass hat,
wear my Mylar gloves on my long hairy arms,
yippee ky yo ky yea, whoo,
yippee ky yo ky yea.

In March we're roping cows on Mars,
by June we're flying to the stars.
Working seven days a week
and I ain't never seen a sheep.
Antelope and floating deer
browsing on the atmosphere.
Yes, I'm an old cowgirl from another world.

That seems to settle the horses down quite a bit. We walk on, dazed by the glittering snow, singing Laura's song over and over until we've memorized the new words.

George sings along, loud as he can, periodically looking back at the horses. He's admitted they're following along sweet as you please.

I unhitch the rope and the horses keep coming after us. "Look," I say to George. "See how they follow along. They don't even care if they're roped now. It's the song. Those are really great words. Don't you think they're really great words?"

"Yeah, they're really great words. Still . . ."

"Still what?" He hesitates and I'm thinking that maybe if we offered him something fine, something like a forever warm bed on a February cold night, maybe then he'd come around. But no.

George looks at me, smiles and says, "It's a good song; it's just that 'Streets of Laredo' is every horse's favorite song."

II. MOVING COWS

Jean Irigaray shows up and tells me he needs some help moving cows—six or maybe nine of his heifers, he says, got through the fence onto Four Mile. Maybe they're in the Bridge Pasture.

"Why you call ranch Four Mile?" he asks, "Forty miles from town. And Bridge Pasture—you got no bridge, that's a dry pasture, no water never in there."

I just shake my head and say, "Never know for naming things. Come on, I'll help you with those cows."

But we don't head for Four Mile right away. We've gotta go to Jean's place and load the saddles onto the old jeep flatbed with the trailer hitch, make sure there's gas, drive south of town to Gladys Esponda's to get the horse trailer, then up to the little pasture that's trapped between two highways to get the horses. We take Trouble, Ms. P,

and Harold. Probably only need two but you never can tell. I don't know which one Jean'll ride. Trouble will take off with him just to prove who's boss. Ms. P will try to bite him or lay down. Harold will just stand there yawning.

Those problems come later. First, we've got to get the horses in the trailer. Trouble's fine, he walks right up and in. Ms. P's a little harder—has to be coaxed. She gets her front legs up but can't seem to see how she's going to get those hind ones over the sill, cracks her shin and leaps forward. OK. Now Harold's the hard one. We have to prop the door so it won't swing in the wind; the rusty noise makes him skitter. Then we have to beg and cajole and tug and push all at once, pick up a foot and set it in the trailer, pick up a second foot and set it in. When I set the second foot down, Harold picks up the first and pulls it back out. I do it again, pushing him forward and picking up a hind foot. For five minutes he stands there like that, three feet in and one kind of hanging in midair. Jean can't believe it. He stands there waiting to see what Harold will do. What Harold does is nothing.

I shrug and, finally, lift that last leg. Then while I hold the leg up, I hit the metal wall of the trailer with the flat of my other hand. When the metal clangs, Harold leaps forward and I close the trailer door.

Now we drive down the gravel road to the Interstate and out of town toward Powder River twenty miles. We get off the Interstate at Schoonover Road and rattle along twenty more miles, six eagles on fence posts, sheep and cows every which way you look, mule deer and pronghorn, a few whitetail. Way out here it's mostly dust and deep eroded washes, sage and greasewood. When we get to Four Mile and turn off the engine, there's a whirring sound like the wind in a distant fence.

No sign of cows. We turn the engine back on and drive, looking for cows. Finally we find them all scattered out along the creek standing in the shade of the cottonwoods, not bunched up like cows ought to be.

We unload the horses, bridle and saddle them and start scooting around moving cows this way and that. Jean goes ahead opening gates we go through and closing them. Every once in a while some cow takes off back where we came from and I go to turn it our way again. I ride around the cows and edge them forward, no rope. Rope's not necessary. Besides, I don't know how to use one.

Finally Jean's cows are back where they belong, and I lift Harold's feet up in the trailer so we can do the whole forty miles in reverse and put the horses back, and take the saddles in, and drop the trailer back at Esponda's, and the Jeep home, and, well, hell, we didn't need these horses, we just wanted them, could have moved those cows by walking slowly behind them way off in the distance.

III. FIRECRACKER

The longer I work with horses the more I find myself speaking of them as if they were people or, if not people, at least as important as people. Perhaps it is self-indulgent in these days of human hunger and disease, wars all over the planet, the pain and death we read about in Zaire, Rwanda, the Middle East, our own rich country. Still, I care for the horses deeply, and it's not as if I imagine them to be metaphors for universal human values. The simple truth is that maybe I do believe they are as important as we are.

Sharing our lives with us, horses come to share our ailments and deaths. They get cancer, for example. It's not even rare. The most common is malignant melanoma. It occurs in all horses,
though mostly in grays. Appaloosas and white horses suffer squamous cell carcinoma, a skin cancer.

All these words. Soon there will be horse oncologists. I don't know if that's frivolous or merely depressing. Oncologists with their words—sonogram, nuclear scanner, gamma scanner, hard radiation machine, lymphoma and lymphocyte—and their diagnoses—equal parts biochemistry, voodoo, and intuition. Right now I'm wound up on this subject, and I lead myself to this story the way I lead a horse toward a trailer inside which he'll ride to the vet's.

It was seventy-five-year-old Jean Irigaray's racer Firecracker, who was twenty-six himself and hadn't been on a track in years. Firecracker's cancer was the melanoma. Jean knew nothing of what was going on inside his horse's body. Our vet, Dr. Tom, explained that most likely the bad cells filled Firecracker, that they had entered the lymphatic system, maybe the kidney and liver. Little could be done though Dr. Tom explained that he could destroy lumps along the skin—cut them out or burn them or freeze them with nitrogen.

Jean was heartbroken—a true breaking of his heart. Human or horse. Jean didn't ask that question. He asked Dr. Tom, "Is nothing more can be done?"

Dr. Tom said that he'd call the CSU vet school in Fort Collins and get back to Jean in a few days. I drove Jean home and, though it was cold, we walked in the pasture. The wind was wailing so that the dried leaves spun and danced like a brainstorm.

"Twenty-six years," Jean said, and I think he meant everything—the pasture, the irrigation ditch and dams, the battered fence posts and worn barbed wire, the way the clouds boil so thick layers shift and fly, opening and closing windows onto the blue. I looked at Jean and realized that these feelings were not some easy sentimentalization—loving an animal because it requires less than loving another person. Instead, I saw that Jean's love of the horses—and mine, too—was a way to have union with another world.

On Wednesday I drove Jean back to the vet's. Dr. Tom felt all over Firecracker's body.

He ran both hands together along the horse's neck, hard questioning fingers, cool from antiseptic. Dr. Tom told Jean there were small bumps everywhere, cancer all over under the skin. I kept quiet, picturing Firecracker's insides as a garden of foul flowers all blossoming at once, inky bloody blooms, poisonous pollen, barbs and ash.

Dr. Tom used an electric knife to cut a walnut-size lump out of the base of Firecracker's neck. Though the horse was anesthetized, he could smell the sizzle of hair and flesh and in terror he bashed against the padded walls of the squeeze chute. Exposed, the lump was a dull rubbery blob, somnolent and benign. Quick-frozen, sliced, and dyed, it was analyzed. Later there were core samples of bone marrow—hollow needles drilled into Firecracker's pelvis, then blood and urine analysis. Dyes were injected into the loose skin between his front legs. All this went on at the university down in Colorado.

"Treatment just like a for a human," they told Jean. "We can do radiation, chemotherapy, treatment just like for a human . . ."

But you can talk to a human being, I thought. And nowadays, on humans even, the plug is pulled, and people go home to die in their living rooms, the busy world at the window, friends and family passing in and out. And wouldn't a horse rather stand in the shade of a cottonwood or lean against the south wall of a shed in a winter wind than die in a building smelling of antiseptic and soap and human?

We're not so good at letting go.

As part of an experiment, CSU paid for most of it. Still, Jean spent $3,000. He told me, "Money don't matter."

For a horse, I thought, but I kept my mouth shut. For fifty years Jean had been one of the stingiest of the carefully stingy Basque ranchers. But when Firecracker was being treated, Jean went down to Fort Collins and stayed in a motel. He asked if I'd drive him and I did and stayed two nights. The motel room was a characterless one with a copy of a western landscape above the bed, two plastic drinking cups sealed in a cellophane bag by the sink, a TV with cable and HBO.

After I left to come home, I pictured Jean there rising alone each day, dressing carefully to go check on his horse. I wanted to go back and stay with him. But I didn't ask, thinking it was just ghoulish. I remembered Jean's wife, dead three years, and wondered if this attention was connected to that death, another way Jean mourned that loss. It was a cheap thought for what mattered to Jean was the horse, the integrity of its life.

"That horse done a lot for me," Jean said. It struck me that what a horse can do for a person—for Jean, for me, for anyone—is exactly what my life in Wyoming had been teaching all along. What a horse can do, a dog, a sheep, a coyote or mountain lion, the snow falling out of the sky. I had somehow never before seen that Jean knew this. How stupid of me. Now I had a glimmer and I knew that I'd never forget.

M I C H A E L   H O U G H T O N

westward

horSepower

SHELBY HEARON

My mother never owned an automobile. To her, full-throttle speed meant loping across an open stretch of west Texas or heading toward the Grand Tetons on horseback. For a woman whose own mother had had to ride in a long skirt, sidesaddle, sitting astride a horse, in lace-up boots and jodhpurs with the bobbed hair of a flapper, was high-powered.

My own first solo experience with a horse took place at Mitre Peak Guest Ranch outside Alpine in the Chisos Mountains the summer I was nine. Having been taught by my mother the rudiments of Western riding—to rein guide, to hug with my knees and urge with my hands, not to use a crop—I was allowed early one August morning to take out my first large, amiable rented bay. What a thrill. Walking right out of the stable yard onto the designated path that led to a vast mountain meadow, I, in my sneakers and corduroy pants, a haircut courtesy of my daddy, felt the master of all I surveyed. I was in charge. When the horse trotted under a low-hanging tree branch in an effort to unseat me, and then tried scraping me off against a fence post, I kept in control. Even when our time was nearly up and I turned her back toward the stable, I managed to hang on during a full all-out gallop.

But just at that moment, a six-foot rattlesnake crossed our path. "Whoa," I screamed, pulling her into a near buck. Terror struck. The horse could toss me off and I could be bitten by the fangs of the rattler and die of the venom, since the first aid rubber tourniquet and razor blade were back in the lodge. The horse could panic and step on the rattler and get bit and go crazy and I'd hit my head on a rock or fall into a cactus bed. But I remembered the rules of the road: pull on the reins lightly with the right hand, hold tight with the knees, pat the broad, smooth chestnut neck with the left hand, and in a soothing voice explain to the horse the best course of action. All went well. The horse came down on all fours, the diamondback rattler, big around as my daddy's arm, slithered slowly off into the low-growing catclaw and thistle, and I wiped my sweaty palms on my pants.

We got back to the corral on time, both of us out of breath and in a bit of a lather. When I slid out of the saddle and dropped to the ground not even using the stirrup, my mother, in her riding trousers, waiting while her horse got saddled, looked very proud. "How did it go?" she asked. I don't know what I told her. Something that signified it was no big deal; a morning canter.

Mother stopped horseback riding in her sixties. Had she come along later, she might well have continued into her eighties. In her last decades, she had to make do with Daddy's Buick Skylark for locomotion. But it never took; she was a dreadful driver. She'd crawl to a stoplight, then, just as the light changed red, try to gun the outsize car into a sprint through the intersection. But with automatic transmission and power brakes, where was the fun? It felt, she said, much like riding a Tennessee Walker back and forth on the lawn.

Sometimes now, when I'm wheeling down the Interstate, a real car junkie, foot on the floorboard, window open, the Green Mountains whizzing by, spring flowers where snow used to be, I think about my mother. And her love for horsepower.

LINDY SMITH

wyoming

Buck (platinum print)

side-view:
a mOther's perSpective

CLEOPATRA MATHIS

My horse-crazy girl grew that way from the very first, pulling herself up on a Fisher-Price, $9.99, plastic pony on wheels before she could walk. Her third word, even before "Mama," was "horse," which arrived immediately after "hot," two utterances to name the great extremes of love and fear. Inspired by pain, in this case the open door of the oven, "hot?" became the question about any unknown object, just as the word "horse" named any four-legged creature. The metal creatures that served as swings in the neighborhood park, the three-foot-high stuffed Clydesdale that my sister sent for her second birthday, the tiny stick-horse ornament that she wouldn't give up after Christmas: these were her first devotions. At three, she found the pony rides at the local fair and would not be tempted by even the merry-go-round, however much I coaxed. The otherworldliness of those painted horses, their dreamy flight, couldn't compete with the scraggly manes she clung to, the earthy smell of the utterly real.

I preferred the fantasy horses myself. The real horse called up dread: the distinct memory of my four-year-old brother unconscious at the feet of a mean animal whose back left hoof had caught my brother cleanly on his bare chest. We had been swimming at the local pool where a couple had tethered their horses. More than my mother's panic and the limp child in the medic's arms, I remember the red imprint of the horseshoe over my brother's heart. Now with even the most trusted animal, I walk at some distance around his hindquarters, and I wince at my daughter's unself-conscious ease as she picks hooves or combs a tail, fussing mildly as the horse steps only inches away from her head.

I've seen the measure of that ease extend to all

manner of horse work. Her hands cup over the reins as gently as if they were eggs, her back achingly straight, as the horse flies over four-foot walls. She manages to make the saddle look like a sofa. But I've also seen her on a horse maddeningly unresponsive, lost to his six years on the track, hell-bent on the cross-country course and my child barely hanging on before the inevitable fall. I've seen her up to the elbows in mucous and blood, seen her plunge her hand into the horse's shoulder, torn to the bone. He had spooked over a trailing lunge line and charged through two barn doors; she was the one to coax him out of the icy field and assist the vet through a long, bitter January afternoon as he sewed her horse back together.

The horse, one learns, is a disorderly, frail creature, brought to an order and strength made legendary. At any moment, any horse may fail, his spindly legs and disease-prone hooves entirely inadequate for the weight they're asked to support. A great, heaving machine powered by a faithful, easily broken heart. Perhaps more than any other animal, the horse is a lesson in contradictions. My daughter, eighteen now, likens the process of training a horse to making art. A sculptor, an essayist, she is in love with shape and form. In her person she tends toward the opposite: messy, disorganized, untimely, and often undisciplined. In a disastrous time we almost lost her to emotional chaos. Early adolescence brought the already tumultuous child to the brink; the suicide of her dear friend on the summer solstice before ninth grade sent her plummeting. She fell past all our efforts into a self-mutilating depression, refusing help so completely that nothing remained but hospitalization.

Through those weeks of therapy, three aspects of her life took shape and guided her: painting, writing, and the desire to be with her horse again. When my daughter was thirteen, we bought an old schoolmaster, a horse who'd had plenty of experience teaching children to ride. Nicky was great-hearted, trusting in the way horses can be when they've had only one or two loving owners. A horse who put aside a physical handicap (nerve damage in his hind) for his love of eventing and, even more, his need to take care of his rider at any cost. Though his passion was to run, though he could go love-crazy rushing the jumps, those who knew horses and saw my concern assured me that if he ever sensed her fear or felt that she was in trouble, Nicky would stop. A good horse takes care of his rider. He saw her safely through the first levels of eventing; we sold him only because he wasn't physically capable of going beyond novice, and I cried. A good horse takes care of his rider. Selling Nicky was possible for my girl only because she had another horse, this one young and green, waiting. Like a drug, he arrived within a half hour of Nicky's departure.

This horse, however, represented a battleground. Just off the track, skeletally underweight, and potentially a knock-out both physically and as an eventer, he was a risk my daughter felt she was ready to take. He would fatten up by at least five hundred pounds, become devoted to the one who gave him kind and consistent care, and suffer one cowardly injury after another. Three years she put into shaping his body and his mind before having to accept that he would never be a successful eventer, never be capable of forgetting whatever demons had plagued him those years he raced.

Whether great terror or great love, something possessed him on the cross-country course that my daughter with all her patience and diligence couldn't overcome. In the end he made her afraid; and in the partnership of rider and horse, fear can only mean failure. And yet, the training of this horse brought her the kind of stability that is born out of constant regard for the well-being of something other than one's self. That love meant so much to her that she almost gave up eventing in order to keep the horse; desire for the relationship outweighed any desire for showmanship. The competition had nothing to do with ribbons, but in forging a bond that could shape her life. In her most critical time, the horse was pure metaphor.

What I have learned through those years with horses is to understand the nature of passion. Passion can be thwarted or perverted, or it can lay the groundwork for commitment. Without the ongoing confrontation and reconciliation of disorder and order, one does not truly ride, one does not make a real poem. In a recent essay, linking the efforts of making art and training a horse, my daughter wrote: "Sculpture, writing, and riding horses enable people to put debilitating emotions into an objective form through example and repetition. An understanding of the artistic process is an understanding of human nature. Once the primary emotion in a behavior is identified, be it a horse's unwillingness to make a tight circle, a character's disability, or the expression on a grimacing clay face, it is possible to begin the process of understanding relationships through contemplating images, whether they are self-generated or simply experienced."

Do I want to say that my daughter's horse saved her life? That the life she lived with horses brought her somewhere she would not otherwise have gone? Clearly, an outer and inner process came together: the horse was a living, breathing representation of her psychological, emotional self. I have no way of knowing how that kernel of strength brought her back, what struggle she overcame. But I do understand that the pull to the barn each morning of the most devastating year, months when she wouldn't even go to school, got her out of bed when nothing else succeeded; that the smell of the fall morning, the cold nose of her horse, the routine of mucking and brushing and saddling up took her to that formal place beyond pain, that realm of feeling in which, in its insistence on distance and dignity, a person can salvage the self.

What I see best in the sharpest eye of my vigilance is not the patchwork of slashes and scrapes along my daughter's arms or the burns on her thighs; what I hear is not an hysterical sobbing. Instead, it's a red October morning up on the hill bordered with birches, and my daughter is already in the ring by the time I walk up. She's got on those clothes, ages old and terribly correct: the hard hat with its velvet ribbon, the tight tan pants and high black boots, all so sweetly formal that I could weep. Anonymously elegant, she is any young rider. She's warming up, the horse snorting, prancing sideways in the new chill of the air; she sits calmly, waiting out his little storm, patient as any mother with her quiet hands. Until her stillness brings him back, until they move as one, his body round, on the bit, in a perfect universe, repeating and repeating.

connemara

I am a great walker, but I like to walk alone. For years I shunned horseback riding, fearing that to ride a horse was akin to walking with a person, making conversation, being polite. I later discovered that to be on a horse is, in fact, to be closer to nature. You become one with the animal: seeing things through the horse's eyes, hearing sounds through the horse's ears. And I like looking down and seeing my feet hooved.

"And then into the deep gorge"

Connemara

Connemara Four

wOrking with hUmanS

PEGGY SUE BROWN

(RITA MAE BROWN'S HORSE)

Humans learn best through repetition. But this is not to say that you can buck your rider off each time s/he misbehaves and they will figure out what they are doing wrong.

Humans like to blame us for their problems. If that fails, they are only too happy to blame another human.

The key is working with them as they are. We can't change them to think like horses.

Starting from the beginning, you must always bear in mind that they are a frail species. They have no hooves. They can't run as fast as a house cat. Their hearing is quite poor and their sense of smell is close to nonexistent.

Another interesting aspect of their anatomy is that their eyes and nose are smack in the middle of their faces. They have such funny flat faces. You and I see and process more information in five minutes than a human can gather in an hour.

What they can do is focus their attention on a specific task. Their eyes are engineered for this purpose. Whereas you and I will move away rapidly from an unfamiliar sound or we'll shy off of an unfamiliar sight, they need the time to focus on the obstacle in order to figure out what it is. Humans need to understand events intellectually. We generally react and figure it out later.

The best way to work in harmony with these two-legged animals is to try to get them to focus on what it is you need them to know. If you lose your temper and buck them off, what they focus on is their fear. But if you patiently lead them to what you need in order to perform at your best, they will figure it out in good time. Once humans learn a lesson, they remember it unless it has to do with their mating behavior, but that is not within the scope of this article.

To illustrate my thesis, let's talk about their legs. A human who doesn't ride will clamber on your back and squeeze your sides with a death grip. They'll either stick their legs way out in front as though on the dashboard of a car or begin to curl them backwards.

This presents an interesting problem. If they don't stop squeezing you have no idea whether to move off or stand still. By now, of course, their hands are up at chest level and that's no help, either.

The secret to teaching them where to put their leg is to stay under them. If they lurch to the left, you scoot to the left. Irritating as this is, over time they will learn to drop their leg by the girth and to stop squeezing so hard because you will have lessened their fear and because staying tense will exhaust them.

The biggest help you can have with a beginner is an experienced human on the ground. For some bizarre reason, many humans think they can get on our backs and ride. They must think it's something like swimming: once you learn you always know how to swim. Nothing could be further from the truth. If it's your misfortune to be stuck with one of these arrogant beginners, try kindness. If they don't learn anything and they don't seek proper instruction in about three months you can then progress through aids. You can toss or bob your head, you can dance sideways. You can refuse to move or you can run off. But aids are only useful if used in succession—from the milder aids to the most severe: planting them with the tulips.

But let's assume you have an intermediate rider on your back, one with a teacher. You like your rider and s/he likes you, but the human won't lower her or his hands. The secret here is not to pull but to slowly lower your head. Sooner or later the reins will slip through their fingers to the desired contact point—a touch in the mouth but no more. Each time they reach their correct contact you soften your stride so it feels better. Humans hate to be jarred about. Each time you soften in response to their good efforts you reinforce the lesson.

If their hands go back up, then be a little straight-legged regardless of gait. When they lower their hands, soften. Do this over and over again until your rider absolutely understands the direct relationship between hands and your way of going.

So many horses have said to me from all disciplines—showing, hunting, barrel racing, saddle seat—that they become distracted when their human babbles. Because humans have such poor senses they had to develop language in order to survive. We communicate easily with ears forward and back, tails swishing, nostrils flaring and the occasional vocal sentence. They run their mouths nonstop. I agree this is distracting. I don't mind a "good girl" or a "whoa," but that's about it. There's not much you can do about a Chatty Cathy except to ignore her or him. My experience is the better the rider the less they talk. Which takes us right back to basics.

They need an educated leg so they can develop educated hands. Each time they put their leg and their hands in the right place, reward them by moving off. Each time they execute a proper slowdown, reward them by a downward transition. When they ask for a smooth stop correctly using their hands and legs, stop.

It's always easier to go from a trot to a canter than from a canter to a trot. Downward transitions are quite difficult for humans. Their bodies arc often a touch too far forward, and when you slow down, instead of staying over your center of gravity, they'll flop on your neck or lurch back, their legs pushing out in front of them, their seat bones driving into the saddle. Irritating as this is, don't speed back up or they'll bob in the opposite direction. If they've fallen back on a downward transition and you go forward in response to their seat they'll be propelled forward. The best thing to do is complete the correct transition, stay in the gait and wait for them to compose themselves.

If they can hear music it helps them. Since our gaits are two-beat or three-beat, hearing the rhythm does help many of them. I prefer they listen to my hoofbeats, but in the interests of making them comfortable I'll listen to Mozart. I don't think any horse is required to listen to Nine-Inch Nails.

To reinforce good behavior, if your human is responsible and worms you monthly, floats your teeth, grooms you daily, and shoes you at four- to six-week intervals given the condition of your hooves, try harder for that human even if s/he is a wretched rider.

Remember to nicker when you see your human. They need to know that you care about them. A few of them actually are worth caring for and they generally bring apples and carrots.

Humans come in all sizes, shapes and ages. Their athletic ability varies greatly, as does ours. If your human is built like Humpty Dumpty, do your best to see s/he doesn't fall off the wall. They can't help being what they are. If you are fortunate enough to have a fit human on your back, with good hands and leg, then perform brilliantly.

It's in your self-interest to make your human look and feel good. Happy humans treat you better, and many of them are so lonely that you are their happiness.

Take into account if your human is under great stress and act accordingly. Sometimes they'll take it out on you. If it's a rare occurrence, forgive them. If it becomes a habit, send them into the stratosphere.

Think of your human as your teammate. That's the winning attitude.

—Peggy Sue Brown
TB/Percheron 161/2H, 10 Years
Position in Life: Field Master

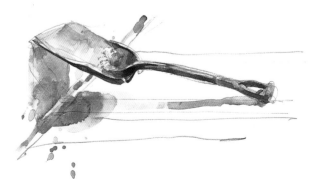

breaking horseS: a Seduction in letter form

PAM HOUSTON

Dear G———,

Let me explain to you the method of using a lunge line in breaking wild horses. Without putting himself at risk, the trainer can attach a long nylon line to one side of the horse's bridle, and stand in the middle of a circle using a whip to make the horse run around him. The horse will buck and kick and rear for a while, it will take her some time to get used to the idea of the circle, but eventually she'll get bored with her own theatrics and simply pull, gently and consistently, against the line on the side of her face.

When she's mastered that, the trainer will try to confuse her by changing the length of the lunge line. She's figured out exactly how many strides it takes to make a circle in the middle range, you see, and when he shortens the lunge line she has to adjust her stride to something more collected and quietly powerful. It is in the small circle where the best trainers make champions, because of their ability to get a horse interested in a new way to run.

The minute the horse gets comfortable inside the smaller circle, the trainer will let out twice as much line as he had her on originally, and she'll charge off with huge strides, confusing the long line with freedom. If she gets out there too far she'll trip and toss her head and he'll see that he's in danger of losing her attention. So he'll pull her back into that mid-range distance where he can exercise the most power for the least expended effort. Because it doesn't require the same level of concentration as the smaller circle, he can stand there for hours watching her run around and around.

The problem with the lunge line method of training is one of psychology and physics. In it, the horse is always moving away from two simultaneous forces; she's pulling against the lunge line at her mouth, and she's running away from the whip behind her heels. If she isn't constantly moving away from what both of the trainer's hands are doing, she is doing it wrong. If she gets tired and tries to come to the center of the circle, he must place the length of the whip between them. If she gets angry and tries to pull the line out of his hand, he must make her move forward by raising and snapping the whip.

When the lunge line training is completed successfully, what it means is that the horse understands perfectly the amount of pressure she must always keep on the line. And when the rider gets on her back for the first time the learning must begin all over again. He will need her to respond to the gentle questions his hands on the reins ask of her mouth. He will need to bend to the pressure of his leg around her flank.

And if they are to go out on the trail together he'll need her to translate the requests of his mind by reading his body. He'll need her to cross rivers and to walk tall through thick brush, to get them out of the dangers that crop up on the trail. She'll need things from him as well, need him to stand calm when a rabbit darts in front of them, when a discarded piece of plastic rattles in an oak tree. She'll need him to forgive her if she forgets for a moment he's up there and runs so hard across a meadow he gets scared he might fall off.

On the trail all the stakes are raised considerably, and it is here that the lunge line training will hurt them most. Because his empty hand will move by habit to put the whip between them, and her head will always be bent slightly against the pressure of a line that exists only in her mind.

And it *is* called "breaking horses," and the reason it is called that is because the term was invented by a man who believed in the myth of possession. This man, whoever he was, believed he was capable of breaking the horse's spirit, of removing all that was wild from her, and he also believed, even more wrongly, that breaking her was the only way he could hold her, when of course,

exactly the opposite was true. That man would be the first to tell you that the horse was only valuable to him when she was strong and free and responded to him out of respect and love and dedication. The minute he "broke" her, he would say (though he'd be wrong, she allowed herself to be broken—which is really like saying she broke herself) he lost interest in her and turned her into a dude horse that old ladies and kids could ride. But of course you know all this.

Let me tell you what happened today. Christine was bent on going riding, and even though this is the city, it is also Texas, so we looked in the phone book and found a dude ranch and signed ourselves up for a three-hour ride. Christine rode a feisty little quarter horse called Charlotte, and I rode a big rangy Thoroughbred/Tennessee Walker cross named Tom. Our wrangler's name was James and he was young and just about as Texan as you can get. And of course we signed papers and everything that said we wouldn't run the horses, but I know Christine better than that, and we weren't twenty minutes into the ride when James made the mistake of going around a different side of a little stand of pines than we did and Christine seized the moment he couldn't see us and belted her horse and we took off at a flat gallop across the top half of this four-hundred-and-some-acre cattle ranch.

A quarter horse is the best horse to have on a trail because she is strong and smart and basically willing to do what you ask her. What a Thoroughbred is good at is putting his head down and running for the finish line, throwing care and caution and sense to the wind, setting his jaw and running, through or around or over whatever might get in his way. It's not his fault. We've bred him for it. And there is nothing I've ever done in my life that is as exhilarating, nothing that is so equally and completely frightening and magical as being on the back of a Thoroughbred when he's in turbo drive. It's as smooth as a Cadillac convertible and much faster. It was the first recreational bargain I made with death, and one of the few I hope to keep making for as long as I live. But I've gotten off track here.

The day went a lot like that. Ten minutes of walk-trot pleasantness and then Christine would bring Charlotte up to where I was and our horses would start bumping shoulders, and I would turn and look at James and catch just the hint of a smile or a shake of his head and that was all we needed to be off again.

Anyway, what I wanted to tell you about was the training, the lessons that took place between me and Tom. The first time he took off on me, I was really scared. He took off like only a Thoroughbred can, and I didn't know him, or the tack I was using, didn't know the terrain. I tried every trick I know to stop him (and I know them all). Constant pressure, intermittent pressure, I tried to turn him hard in a tight circle, tried shouting *whoa, whoa, whoa* at every possible voice level, tried even to kick him to attention (very poor horsemanship), and finally, after crossing three streambeds, clattering over two very nasty rock outcroppings, and shaving off about fifteen trees branches with various parts of my body, I found a big canyon wall to run Tom into.

"Don't let that horse put his head down on ya," James said when he caught up to us that first time, "That horse puts his head down, and you're just flicked."

The second time we took off I played it a little different. I let him run as fast as he wanted until we got to a place that was steep and rocky. And then I hauled back on the reins one time, said *whoa* once loud and sat back hard in the saddle. Tom stopped on a dime.

After that we came to a big open meadow. James said we couldn't go down there because it was the horses' winter pasture and they would get a little crazy in it, and I asked if I could go down for ten minutes by myself and work with Tom. I went down into the meadow and galloped him around in tight tight circles, but every time he'd stop fighting me, I'd drop the reins a little, and let him make the circle just a little more wide.

I talked to him with my legs the whole time, too (and this is where English-schooled riders have the advantage because horses respond so naturally to the legs' direct language rather than, say, the indirect language of the neck rein or the whip), asking for the gallop, and then asking for control (not my control, of course, but his, asking him to control his own gallop), showing him that asking for speed and asking for control are not opposites, that they can be the same question asked with one movement of the leg, and you see that's why the legs are so important because in the same movement they ask for something from the horse, they also make a promise. They say you can trust me. They say I'm asking you to gallop with me, but I'm also telling you at every second that I'm right here with you to help you have the courage to gallop.

The horse holds the rider up, it's true, but the rider holds the horse . . . in, or together. This is especially true when a horse and rider are out alone, because horses are herd animals and they need that constant contact of the leg then much more than most riders know.

Before too long we were galloping big circles around the whole meadow.

Christine told me that the whole time we were

down there James was saying, "Any second now Tom's going to come flying over that hill dragging that little gal behind him." And I did let him out as we ran the last length of the field back to where Christine and James were standing. But I wasn't hanging on for my life anymore. I was flying along right with him.

It was, from then on, one of the best rides ever on a horse I didn't know. And we did give James a really big tip.

And of course we are talking here about the ability of the trainer to teach, and the horse's ability to learn, as well as the trainer's ability to learn and the horse's ability to teach, and that is what makes horseback riding different from tennis or skiing, that there are two wills constantly engaged and those four learning situations are always and must be at every moment inextricable.

And of course a horse tests his trainer, he tests her every minute, he reads her fears straight through her body like no human being ever could, he senses any momentary inattention and capitalizes on it. He sometimes pretends to be much less intelligent than he is, he walks into a hole or gets caught up in barbed wire, and I don't know why exactly. Maybe he likes watching her hands gently separate the barbs from his fetlocks. Maybe he recognizes this as a tremendous act of love.

And of course they talk to one another, and most days they reach an understanding, and he becomes more human and she more equine, which doesn't take all that much becoming, because if she didn't have an equine spirit she wouldn't have become a horse trainer, and if he didn't have a human sensibility, he wouldn't be her chosen horse.

And she does get tired, but not of him, or even of the training, but of falling down all the time in the same place.

And though he's been tricked (not by her, but by something bigger, some universal law of order that is questionable but stronger than them) into believing that she's the one who's holding the lunge line, the simple laws of nature are that because of the different ways they are put together, one well enough placed kick can break her arm into nineteen pieces.

And the one thing he really understands about her (and it's both the reason he sometimes bucks her off and the reason he'll walk through fire for her) is that what she wants most of all, what all the years of training have shown her, is the possibility of never again needing to use the whip.

Did I tell you that Jerry Jeff Walker signed my blond leather coat?

Did I tell you about Gruene, Texas, and the oldest dance hall in the state?

Did I tell you that in everything I see that moves me . . . in the young girl at the grunge bar with magenta hair and ten nose rings, in the tall young blues singer in a band called Joe Teller who wailed into the microphone and wrapped his arms around it like an invisible woman and then walked offstage saying, "I hate this fucking six-string, I hate this fucking club, and I hate all you fucking people," in the third verse of "Mr. Bojangles," in the deep-set lines on Jerry Jeff's life-worn face, in the paler lines of clouds in the sky last night behind a lone Texas windmill, in the scrubby cedars and naked gray rocks of the canyons of the Triple Creek Ranch, in the first surprise of speed in sixteen hands of horseflesh underneath me, in the slowing of that same horse, in the giving in. In all of these things and at every moment, I see my love for you.

city horses

It doesn't take much to find evidence of the horse's importance in history. Most cities are littered with monuments with some historical figure astride his trusty steed. Before the inanimate, noisy, land- and air-polluting automobile, people had love affairs with their horses, and a few still do.

The horse and dedicated owner can still be found in the present-day cement cosmopolis. The city horse is a different breed, so to speak, than his rural cousin. Often dressed up and ready to go out on the town, it is his path that I cross most often.

London Whitehall Horseguard

Brussels Horse and Thief

New York City Policeman

The City Horse

angel foot: a double portrait

TESS GALLAGHER

"I am almost afraid to write down this thing"

—James Wright

If she were only a memory I could call her back— horse of my childhood who continued with me into womanhood. But she outstrips memory, runs through my veins, pulses luxuriously like the still yet trembling frissure of haloed light around a full moon on a blue-black night above hemlocks.

I can't say her. We simply coexist in an ongoing state of suspended approach across space and time, and we are as far from language as a hummingbird is to a windmill.

Our two hearts were skywriters for a time against and above the earth. With her I had hoofbeats like muffled breaths pressed into the ground. A windy mane caressed, then stung my cheek.

What did she have in me? An awkwardness she converted to an extension of her own ungaugeable immersion, for her mind inhabited an immensity of nomadic space I could only sense when she carried me on her back in that now vanished space of my grandfather's thousand-acre farm in the Missouri Ozarks. She had my caresses and my awkward wishfulness to please her, to respect and deserve her beautiful presence, the gaiety of her head toss and prance.

There is probably an intricate history of the horse as gift—the significance of the handing over of this animal person to person. I think of the Duke of Lorraine and his gift to Joan of Arc of a black horse. She was later given another black horse by D'Alençon to add to horses the king had given her—five warhorses and more than seven trotting ponies. It is astonishing to the child, this tie of the living gift, the union of animal and human spirit: for this was the way Angel Foot did not *come* into my life, but was presented, as if we had been preordained for each other, in a manner not unlike that through which Dalai Lamas are at once discovered and recognized. And though we were often to be separated through force of circumstance, we managed to sustain—what else can I call it—friendship across thirty years.

Her mother was named Diamond for the white gleam inscription showing through her black forelock. Angel Foot's sire was a black-on-black stallion named King whom I only saw once and who resembled the purebred Arabians still raised at El Zahraa that I admired later in picture books. Their handsome lineage goes all the way back to the pharaohs, and before that to the wild high desert of the Arabian peninsula. From this stallion my grandfather said Angel got "spunk and stamina." (My people would sooner have had horses than cattle

and knew how to gauge them.) In her carriage she gave off a hush of nobility, an aura of secret entitlement.

From Diamond she had gentleness. Her fine gaze seemed to flow out from her with mysterious shadowy sweepings like lantern light in a field. She more than saw me: She *shone onto me* and blotted me out and into her consciousness which, like mine, was exuberance coiled into an electric expectation. We were two beings waiting to expend ourselves in motion across space. I have her yet, though she is fourteen years dead. She is melded onto my will, my sense of what it is to slip humanness and inhabit myself as a keen yet boundless going forth, for always we ventured, sought out, explored, traversed, passed under boughs, across meadows, through the river, came to a chilly halt before a cave.

She was the gift of my uncle and my maternal grandfather, but she had been hand-raised for me by my Uncle Porter. "Your filly is born," he wrote from Windyville, Missouri. "I have named her Angel Foot for the white on her hind foot where God must have held onto her when he dipped her into the black." This magical notion of Angel's creation lodged in me like the notion of absent peoples inside the land that had occurred to me when I saw my grandfather pluck stone arrowheads from the furrows as he plowed with his team horses, Daisy and Dolly. He collected these arrowheads for me in a Mason jar. Their missing shafts are like the invisible slope of memory down which one is always sliding in a half-controlled hopefulness of finding what is unaccountably lost, necessarily lost. I search language now for that shorn force which projected that horse, that girl through the brooding walnut grove in August.

For it was always summer when we were most likely to meet. With a canvas canteen strapped to our truck, my family crossed the country from Washington State to Missouri. I was twelve when I saw Angel that first time. Later I would have her also in winter and by moonlight in spring.

Can a step be delicious ever again after feeling in sun-shock her forehooves break the sugared snow-crust of the Jericho? The Jericho was a wide wagon path that passed through a scrub oak forest that opened onto a small enclosed meadow, only to close again fifty yards on in forest. Angel's ears would swivel with alertness as we approached this meadow, since often we would meet deer there. For her it must have been like coming onto some quicksilver fear-garden as the sprung leaps of the deer carried themselves as glazings of passionate flying into sudden absence. Then, hanging in the air before us like aftermath of thunder, would be the over-emptiness of their escape. My legs pressed to Angel's sides may never again know such trembling as in that long unraveling, that startle-pitched moment when we broke the solitude of the clearing; in that instant the deer became vanishings, as of ourselves, but a vanishing that also prolonged us in some unforgettable double-headed ambush of the world's peace.

In short, with Angel I was alive beyond aliveness. Each instant lay ready to ignite, to powder up, to strike itself dumb with liquefied time pouring in sudden gouts from any surface. Nothing could be taken for granted when I was astride her, except her will to carry me like a strange loving cup of water she was determined not to spill.

She had a great sense of humor and could initiate a dare. Once, paying no more attention to me than a twig in her forelock, she pretended, at a gallop, not to know we were approaching a barbed-wire fence and ran us almost into it before she smugly stopped on a dime with her nose at the wire. Like a Spanish dancer she could slap her heels down in fateful, clamorous silence: "So there!"

At other times I learned from her what was reasonable. Her lack of tolerance for any imposition on her good will and energies was as fine a gift as anyone has given me. Because language held little sway with her, our communion centered in touch and intuition, in responsiveness to the moment. As with sight-reading sheet music at the piano, one had to be both in the moment and mentally gliding ahead of it, looking to see what could loom in the pathway of her more supple imagining. Still, she was not one of those neurotic horses who turns the world into a warehouse of dangling skeletons. She was full of balance and equanimity, which made her an excellent mount for cattle-herding. My uncle and I often marveled at her ability to outthink a breakaway heifer.

Angel had a wonderful single-foot gait that cost her nothing and that Uncle Porter claimed was bred into her. She could maintain it over the roughest ground, and she took such pleasure in it that she was unwilling to break stride for pigsty or goatherd. This gait, akin to Zeno's moving-yet-still arrow, caused me to feel I was levitating above the swimming curvature of her motion under me. It was like having the earth and letting it go in a simultaneous gesture. Call it the sensation of unearthly-earth. I think of it as a profound unrecorded state of agreement, those timeless apostrophes aboveground together.

How much mystery did she draw from her name? Angels, after all, were supposed to be winged divine intermediaries, God's messengers. But they were also on loan to us as our special guardians. What was her message if she was a messenger? The ever-expanding invisible boundaries of our trust? That the entwined creations of our journeys could be revisited in later times, when I was humbled and adrift, like resilient shrines of mystery?

And how did she guard me? In letting me know by example that love was no human prerogative? For besides herself, she gave me the animals and birds anew, and the very aliveness of the ground under me. It strikes me that there is a reason for the term "horse sense" and that having it is more useful than "common sense." Horse sense maintains a high notion of the ridiculous, of what is beneath dignity. And to know where dignity resides is to spare oneself the trouble of many noxious encounters.

"Nothing shines like a black horse," my uncle would say when I had brushed Angel until sunlight clanged its noon-high gong in rivulets along her muscles. Then I would braid red ribbons into her mane and forelock. On went her red saddle blanket, then the tooled black western saddle. I would have salvaged one of Mother's stylish hats out of the thirties from the attic. When I climbed up, we cut a figure: memory adores a girl on horseback. Why not recall Joan of Arc as remembered by Guy de Laval in a letter to his mother: "armed all in white, except her head, with a little ax in her hand, on a great black charger," and further, how the horse, with divine discretion, no doubt, would not let her mount until she led it to the cross.

It is possible that my longing toward discovering forms for feminine heroic possibilities derives from having seen the world from the back of a horse at an early age: but also from some instinctive need to imagine myself in largesse, as seen in the posture of one on a moving throne, not unlike the Celtic goddess Epona, on the back of a horse. Or again like Joan of Arc, painted by Deruet among dashing cavaliers.

Shortly before he was unexpectedly to die, my friend Jim Sorcic asked for a photograph of me on the back of Angel Foot, for I had told him I planned to call a book of poems *My Black Horse* after her. Jim was waiting in Alabama for a lung transplant that might have saved his life. But while he waited he needed spirit-signs. I think this photograph struck him as just such a portrait, marshaled at once with daring and power and joy. I hope it gave him peace and courage to gaze there since messages often comfort as much as they ward off harm. Our message was simple and he needed it: *with, with, forever with!*

And even now she would know me if I came to the edge of her field and called to her. She would gravely swing her swoon of a neck round to fix me in her world-glossed sight. Then, her tail lifted and spread, she would jigsaw over to me as if she had won me at some lottery of expendable humans, hiding all the while her tender eagerness for reunion by walking the velvet cathedral of her beautiful black head to me the last few angel steps.

goldart

HENRY TAYLOR

A few years ago, a couple of other poets and I took our turns before an audience, talking about how our teaching and writing styles had evolved, diverged, coincided, helped or hindered each other. I had prepared remarks, but suddenly, there before an audience, I realized for the first time the significance of my earliest teaching experience, which was equestrian. When teaching riding, it is important to be audible, and experience shows that people on the ground have to speak right up if they are to be audible to people on horseback. It has something to do with the wind past the ears, the sounds of hooves and leather in the more immediate surroundings. Some people, seeing a riding class for the first time, think the teacher is shouting unnecessarily. It is also important that students react as quickly as possible to instructions; you can prevent a fall if your student can stay in touch with what you are saying, even as something is going wrong. So I came to the college classroom having taught in a loud voice, in expectation of immediate obedience. Some people will doubtless opine that this is poor preparation for a writing teacher; I am tempted to suggest that you not mock it till you try it, but honesty requires me to admit that I have tried to soften the drill-sergeant image somewhat.

Nevertheless, it remains fundamental to my life that my knowledge of poetry is more tentative than my knowledge of horses, though by now it is probably no less thorough. I have only rarely learned a poem, or something about a poem, with the immediacy and force that characterized many of my equestrian lessons.

Take, for example, the fear of undeserved good luck. A complex emotional and intellectual apprehension with which many writers are familiar, to which I came most memorably one afternoon during a fit of temporary insanity—or hubris. The summer that I was eighteen, I took over from one of my sisters the training of a capable but difficult mare. She was intelligent and physically quick—a fine combination of attributes, you might think, unless you already know that smart horses expend much of their intellectual energy trying not to do what they are being asked to do. Goldart, as she was called, had discovered that she could unload my sister almost at will, particularly in front of a jump, where she could stop with almost supernatural suddenness.

Her background—that assortment of innate and acquired factors so important to Southern gossip and narrative—was unusual. A friend of ours named Russell Dart had got hold of a palomino stallion of unknown provenance, and spent a few months trying to get along with him. He was large and athletic, a talented jumper, and seemed mostly willing. But located here and there over the portions of his body that a person could reach from the saddle, there were strange—buttons, you might call them, hidden switches that, when pressed, would cause him to kneel, rear up, fall down and play dead, or something equally irrelevant. There was no one to tell Dart where those things were, even after he discovered that the horse had been one of Trigger's many stand-ins. So he sold the horse to a man who had the time and the inclination to seek out the pressure points and divest them of their significance. Throughout this brainwashing the horse never lost his quickness; it eventually became possible to show him as a jumper, but when he stopped at a jump, he was so quick and so dirty that I would not have believed it if I had not seen it for myself. One afternoon at the Warrenton Horse Show, I watched him unload three of the best show riders in Virginia, because they could not doubt, from the way he was moving, that he was about to jump—but he wasn't. Before Dart got rid of him, he sired Goldart, whom we bought when she was about three.

She had her sire's evasive quickness, but she also seemed to know when it might not work; if either my father or I got on her, she would start looking around for things to jump over. A few weeks of work reinforced her in the conviction that it would be better not to stop with me. At this point, unfortunately, I began to override her; I kept her between my hands and legs, building in her gradually the notion that she did nothing on her own. In a few weeks she had quite thoroughly learned the sequence of sensations in her mouth, back, and sides that I wanted her to associate with jumping; she got so she would jump over three feet of empty air whenever I asked her to. It was fun to do that while galloping across a field, a few lengths ahead of other riders who would immediately pull up, looking for the strand of wire they thought I must have seen. This overriding is not usually a good idea, but perhaps only those who have done it can appreciate the complexity and interest of conversations between horse and rider, carried out beyond the realm of words, but not beyond the realm of question and answer, doubt and reassurance, disagreement and agreement, even meditation and interjection. Dangerous as the development of this overdependence is, however, things can be worse. One day I was seized by the aforementioned insanity, a late-teenage recklessness with the power I seemed to possess.

I wanted to know whether Goldart would attempt more than she could do.

The cruelty of that question is still painful to me, though I am talking about something that happened almost forty years ago, to someone so remote from me that I would not dream, for example, of revising his writing, even though the law allows me to, and though I have many times asked myself to do more than I could do. For example, there is wishing to undo what happened next. I would even settle for a general belief that I have made this up.

I rode her at the side of a ten-foot straw rick and asked her to jump over it, fully aware that only two horses in recorded history have jumped higher than eight feet.

She galloped toward it with the eager steadiness that I had long since learned to recognize as unshakable purpose: she thought we were going over it. The straw was old, and gave deeply, so her legs plunged in and stuck there for a moment that I have lately recalled as I have read about Velcro jumping. At last, though, she pried herself loose and we made our way back down the side of the straw rick without mishap. She must have concluded, if she considered it at all, that she had done what she was supposed to do, because the episode appeared to have no effect on her willingness to negotiate reasonable obstacles—and I mean reasonable for her, whose abilities were unusual. From then on, I had to ride her as if I did not remember that I had violated her trust, and kept it anyway.

That was not the reason that our association was somewhat brief as these things go—a few months, I think—and it ended on a much happier note. I began to let her make her own decisions, and we won our last competition because of mutual trust and understanding.

The competition was a junior jumper class under international rules such as the Olympians follow, and I had prepared for it assiduously. The course, a dozen jumps or combinations, was hard to remember, but I had it grooved. (Going off-course was something I did more often than I enjoy remembering.) What I did not know was that the ring was so small, and so closely surrounded by spectators, that Goldart could not believe she could gallop in it. All day, in working hunter classes, I tried to get her out of a trot, greatly to the amusement of the crowd and my competitors. Late in the afternoon, while she was on the van nibbling a little hay, and my father and I were chatting about this and that in the shade nearby, a man we knew from these venues, who showed a number of jumpers under his daughter's courageous guidance, came by and asked my father if he'd like to come see the horse that was going to win the Junior FEI class. "I don't need to move," my father said, glancing into our van. "I can see her just fine from here." People who think "parent" is a verb might say that he should not have increased the pressure on me that way, but the effect was soothing; it increased my confidence to know that he shared it.

After dark the lights made the ring seem larger, but not large enough. I let Goldart trot, while my father, as I later learned, sat in the stands shaking his head and saying, "He'll never make it." I could tell, somehow, that we were going fast enough—FEI rules penalize not only jumping faults, but time faults, incurred for exceeding a posted time allowed. We maintained a good pace, and she jumped clean, and all I had to do was remember the course. Ours was the only round with no time faults and no jumping faults. A few months later, we sold Goldart, and her new owner claimed to get along with her very well. I have never persuaded myself that I deserved this happy outcome; it reassures me to note that Goldart did.

IVARS HEINRIHSONS

suite of paintings

Aura (White Horse), 1992

Restraint of the Horse, 1978

Night Horse, 1989

paperback rider
an interview with dick francis

FRANZ LIDZ

The steeplechase horses at Newton Abbot Racecourse look like tiny figures in a landscape by J. M. W. Turner as they take the far jumps over gorse-packed fences. Dick Francis and I watch them float easily over hedges. As afternoon shadows stretch across this dowdy old country racecourse in Devonshire, a fourteen-year-old bay gelding named Skipping Tim wins going away.

"Did you bet on him?" I ask.

"I never bet," Francis says. "If I did, I'd only watch one horse. I prefer to watch the tactics of all the jockeys."

The British steeplechase season is just opening. And Francis, once England's champion steeplechase jockey and now the prosperous, popular author of mystery thrillers, is on this day about 90 percent rider and 10 percent writer. "Riding was my first love," he says. "It's lovely when you're on a good horse and seeing the fence in front of you. Nothing could be more satisfying. But when you're on a bad horse it's not so good."

His worst race, and unhappily the most famous and unforgettable, came on a good horse, the Queen Mum's Devon Loch, in the 1956 Grand National at Aintree, Britain's greatest race. Francis and Devon Loch were maybe 100 feet from winning the first Grand National for the royal family in more than half a century when the horse inexplicably fell, splayed out on the track like a drunk after a barroom brawl. The mishap before 250,000 race fans was simply devastating, a kind of stomach-wrenching, disastrous embarrassment.

It still pains Francis to talk about the race—which may explain why Aintree has never been the setting for one of his thrillers. He doesn't say much about Devon Loch, either. The only time he mentions the horse, he's sotto voce, saying "D. L."

✄

I'd first met Francis fifteen years ago in the Jockey Club, just off the lobby of the Ritz-Carlton in Washington. He and his wife, Mary, were having a spot of breakfast. "I had a day's hunting with the Green Spring Valley Hunt," Dick said. "I'm having a day with the Elkridge-Harford Hunt next week. One of the masters is Mrs. Schapiro. And she's mounting me."

"You'll have to stop saying that," Mary cautioned mildly. "She's 'lending you a horse.'"

Dick loyally ordered an English muffin, Mary a blueberry muffin.

"We live in a village called Blueberry," she remarked." Only it's spelled B-L-E-U-B-U-R-Y," Dick said. "In Oxfordshire. I've got some land, used to be more. My son trains horses. He sends his horses to my place for their summer vacation, or to recover from injuries. We have two sons, Merrick, the older, who is the trainer, and Felix, a former schoolteacher and a very good shot with the rifle."

I asked if that's where he got the idea for *Twice Shy*, in which two brothers confront a violent killer.

"No," he said with a laugh that made his shoulders rattle. "I didn't actually model the heroes on my sons."

And he reversed the roles in *Twice Shy:* The younger brother was the horse trainer, the older the teacher-marksman. "Merrick trains at Lambourn, a famous racing village in England," he said. Then he and Mary ambled off through the restaurant, and caught a cab to the racetrack.

✄

In the years since, Dick and Mary have moved to the Cayman Islands, and Dick has produced fifteen more books, all of which have been translated into more than thirty languages, including Mandarin, Bantu, and his native Welsh. "I'm embarrassed to say I don't understand a word of Welsh," Francis informs me at Newton Abbot. "It's a mystery to me."

At seventy-seven, Francis looks fit, tough and sinewy as a hawthorne staff, a bit knobby about the chin and creased at the arch of the eyes, but not much heavier than when he was a jockey. I tell him he looks especially good for a man who's broken a fair number of bones in his body above the waist: skull, wrist, arm, and three vertebrae. He tells me he has broken his nose five times, collarbone twelve, more ribs than he ever bothered counting.

"Nothing serious," he says. "I never broke my leg. That's serious because you're on crutches and in plaster." A bit irritating, that, as one of the heroes of his novels might say. They, too, tend to be resilient ex-steeplechase jockeys who've been banged up a bit.

Dressed nattily in a brown sport coat and tattersall trousers, Francis is a curious and observant fellow, confident and yet disarmingly self-deprecating. When I ask him why he started writing, he says, "Because the carpets were getting thin, and my sons needed educating."

We walk out to the Tattersalls enclosure. It's a lovely day. We talk about thoroughbreds, bookmakers, and how a good many of his books are uncomplimentary to racing. Horse owners and trainers are often insensitive crooks, jockeys throw races, and in *Decider* the villains own the track. I say, "Do you get much flak from horse people?"

"I once asked a steward if he thought my books were doing racing an injustice. `Oh, no,' he said, `your books attract people to racing.'"

Francis pulls out a notebook and jots down a few words. "I wrote nothing until I was thirty-six," he says. That's when he began his memoir, *The Sport of Queens*. Upon its publication in 1957, he was offered work as a racing columnist for the *Sunday Express*. "At that point Mary said, 'Why don't you try your hand at a novel?' Since then I've written roughly a novel a year, except in 1965, when I wrote two."

Over a lunch of sliced tomatoes, Francis details his writing routine. "It never varies," he says. "I start each novel in early January, writing in longhand in a large notebook." One draft. "I never do more than one. And I write in pencil, so if I don't like the look of a sentence, I can rub it out immediately." Once he likes the shape of a sentence, he doesn't change it again. "It takes me a long time to think of the main character, then nearly as long to think of the name I'm going to call him. I have the main plot in my mind and a lot of the story before I put pencil to paper. Then I start, and I go on and on. I have the dirty deed in my mind as well. And there is nearly always a dirty deed."

He types the final manuscript into a word processor. His publisher in London, Jenny Dereham of Michael Joseph Ltd., flies down to the Caymans to collect it in mid-May. "She always says if I meet her at the airport she knows it's finished," says Francis. "If my wife meets her, I'm probably struggling with the last few paragraphs."

Though they return to England several times a year to visit their sons, Francis says he and Mary spend most of their time in the Caymans; Mary is bothered by asthma, and English weather doesn't suit her. The couple also keeps an apartment in Fort Lauderdale, but so far Dick has not been tempted to write about the Florida turf scene. "I don't know enough about the inside of American racing," he says. In fact, only one of his books—*Blood Sport*—is largely set on American turf. "Mary and I did the research for that novel by bus," he says. "We went to dude ranches in Wyoming and Arizona." The frugal couple toured the country by Greyhound on $90 passes. "We covered 7,500 miles in three weeks!" Francis crows.

Francis says Mary provides much of the research, in addition to offering editorial guidance. She took up painting for *In the Frame*, photography for *Reflex*, and learned to fly for *Flying Finish*. She wound up owning an air-taxi company in Oxford, England—which she sold in 1976—and wrote a book of her own, *The Beginner's Guide to Flying*. "We're a writing team," Dick says. "Mary reads my work every day. We discuss plot lines and how to get certain characters out of certain situations. I only wish she'd let me put her name on the books."

No elegant stylist, Francis propels his tales with plain, economical prose. C. P. Snow, the celebrated English writer, once praised Francis's "considerable inventiveness, both in plot and in technical devices, so that on superficial levels his books would compare favorably with the James Bond stories." Like 007, Franciscan heroes are chivalrous, tenacious, and self-reliant—a bit like their creator. "I try to give them characteristics I'd want," he says. "I'd hate to make a hero of someone I'd disapprove of."

I ask Francis which character he created most in his own image. "Sid Halley," he says excitedly. Sid is the former jockey with an artificial hand who appears in both *Odds Against* and *Whip Hand*. From memory, Francis quotes a passage in *Whip Hand*: "I could still feel the way I'd moved with the horse, the ripple of muscle through both the striving bodies, uniting in one. I could still feel the irons round my feet, the calves of my legs gripping, the balance, the nearness to my head of the stretching brown neck, the blowing in my mouth, my hands on the reins. . . . Living, of course, was quite different. One discarded dreams, and got dressed, and made what one could of the day."

I read a passage aloud from *Bonecrack* and ask if it could serve as Francis's epitaph: "Give me a horse to ride and a race to ride in and I don't care if I wear silks or pajamas. I don't care if there's anyone watching or not. I don't care if I don't earn much money or break my bones or if I have to starve to keep my weight down. All I care about is riding and racing and winning if I can."

Francis smiles upon hearing his own words. "Yes, riding was my first love," he says. "It's lovely when you're on a good horse, seeing the fence in front of you. Nothing could be more satisfying." He quickly adds, "But writing has its compensations. When a race is over, it's gone for good. A book remains."

As Francis orders a lager, I think about how I can bring Devon Loch up tactfully. I say: "I've heard the Queen Mother is a big fan of yours."

"Oh, yes!" Francis says. It turns out the Queen Mum and the Queen often invite Francis to join them in the Royal Box at the many racecourses the family frequents. Francis reciprocates by hand-delivering advance copies of his books to the royals. Sometimes the Queen Mother even offers a critique. "Aren't your novels getting a little bloodthirsty?" she chided him after reading *Bonecrack*. Francis replied gently, "I hope, Ma'am, you'll still enjoy them."

Francis hasn't touched his dish of tomatoes. A waiter comes by and takes it away. Francis orders another lager and brings up the D. L. thing himself. "The fall remains one of racing's great mysteries," he says wearily. "Devon Loch was uninjured. Personally, I think Devon Loch simply recoiled from the roar of the crowd anticipating the royal family's victory. It was a terrible thing to have happen."

Francis says he rode and won three days later. He went on to win eight more by the end of the season, including the Welsh Grand National, which is something like winning the Arkansas but not the Kentucky Derby. He says he retired the next year. He was still winning, but he was thirty-six and getting on for a steeplechase jockey. He didn't bounce back as quickly after a fall. He'd been Britain's champion jockey in the 1953-54 season. He didn't have anything to prove. But he would never win a Grand National.

"Well," he begins, "I wish I could have gone on riding and ridden in it again the following year. I'd have loved to try to put the record straight." The slightest of smiles creases his brow. "Ah . . . I look on it now as a blessing in disguise. If it hadn't happened, I might never have written a book."

the pOwer of horSes

JOY HARJO

I come from a people who are taught to forget nothing. Every thought, every word, every song or horse that existed makes a mural of existence that gives form to this one we find ourselves in. The construction of a word will draw forth the thing itself. The flank of a horse or the nicker will bring the horse into view. One horse will invoke the history and mythical construct of horses. The love of horses will make horses appear, as will the fear of them. The heart is perhaps the first horse, making its way from the collective imagination, from the center of the earth to the lands of my people in the southeastern part of what is now called the U. S., into Oklahoma, and the late twentieth century.

I am of the Muscogee (or Creek) people. We know about horses, though we are not classified as horse people like many of the Plains tribes, nomadic peoples for whom the horse became crucial to the shape of culture. (The Muscogee word for horse is *rokko*, which means "big deer.") The Muscogee, like many other Indian nations, quickly adopted horses for their usefulness and beauty. Most of the horses that made it into our lands were descendants of Andalusian stock brought to Florida from the Spanish.

I grew up hearing stories of horses and our family's relationship to them. There was no long inclusive narrative, rather pieces of evidence that surfaced in the mundane world, linking the history of horses with our family. Identified with these stories was an ornately beaded saddle blanket that had belonged to my grandmother Naomi Harjo, my father's mother. It was an item acquired through trade during one of my grandmother's many travels. It is from the last century, from a Plains tribe, the beading intricate, nearly perfect in predominantly red and white, decorated with pieces of red, white and blue army ribbon and small bells of brass that are now half missing. This beaded blanket linked my family to the meaning of horse, and it also became a means to know my grandmother, to know of her love of horses. It also came to represent the spirit of my family. The name Harjo means "so brave you are crazy": a warrior name given for bravery, a name to live up to in these strange times. My grandmother Naomi Harjo was also a painter. My favorite painting, which graces each place I live, is a near life-size portrait of Osceola, a leader of the Muscogee people, who never surrendered to the U. S. government.

My grandmother died shortly after my father was born, leaving him to mourn for her the rest of his life. He was in need of horses, but times had changed and the many horses he would have accumulated through family and bravado were replaced by cars, particularly Cadillacs and Ford pickups, which he repaired, shined and talked to for hours as he nursed a beer for comfort. Later I mourned his departure from our family by divorce, though in truth it was a relief because his pain was a whirlwind twisting in our house. He left the horse blanket, accidentally I think, because he took every other piece of art that his mother had created or traded for in her many travels. In the chaos that followed his departure, as if the winds had tossed every piece of chance and dumped them, I made sure the blanket was visible to me. Often it was stacked behind colored plastic laundry baskets overflowing with laundry to be ironed, one of my many tasks. I struggled to find beauty in the sweep of brutality that followed in the wake of loss and found

comfort in the horse blanket, in thinking about the horses, about the appearance of beauty in the heart despite the lack of it otherwise. Did my father look to it for sense, find meaning in the pattern woven with beads, decorated with bits of ribbon and brass, as I did? Did he lose that sense of pattern when he left us?

The beauty of this blanket was meant to decorate the back of a horse and said something about the family, the woman who beaded it. There was a horse it was intended for, a horse who had dignity and caused the blanket to be beaded for it, a horse who was loved and whose smell would carry a child into the memory of songs, tall grass and a wealth of beauty. When I was near that blanket I knew that someone had graced this earth who had brought beauty here. I knew something of the soul of my grandmother. I missed her, as my father did. And I missed the horses, smelled them as they entered my room in the dark, nickering softly.

The history of horses from my father's family is a trail deep, wide and mysterious. It begins even before the Spanish because there were horses on this continent in the long before. They appeared and disappeared like the wave of the Ice Age. The antecedents of horses are spaces akin to black holes in the whirling air around us that give rise to the creations of those beautiful animals we know as horse, some of them as relatives. Our destinies intertwine.

One summer afternoon I drove my Aunt Lois Harjo around the back roads of the Creek Nation of Oklahoma. At every bend in the road, at every creek, at every river, was an occasion for a story. The density of human character thickened, deepened with each permutation of flaw and shine. We drove the roads that were created by trails made by horses, long before cars, which wasn't that long ago. Occasionally horses still cantered these roads. They more often met the sound of my truck with stares and turns of the head from the fields of rich earth spread out on either side of the road.

I can remember a wood frame house that came into view at the side of the road and how it disappeared with steady velocity, as my aunt told me about a black horse belonging to Monahwee, her great-great-great-grand-father, a Muscogee leader who fought fiercely against the removal of our tribe from the southeastern part of the U. S. to Oklahoma. This horse was legendary in beauty and speed, as was Monahwee's ability with horses. He was known for his magic with animals, his ability to commu-nicate with them. My aunt Lois reminded me that he was also gifted in the ability to travel on a horse in an unusual manner. He could leave for a destination at the same time as everyone else, but arrive long before it was humanly possible, a feat impossible in linear time. As she spoke I saw Monahwee on his black horse in the rolling hills of what is now known as Alabama and Georgia. Maybe that moment is the seed that sent me to our homelands years later, to see this place that had everything to do with our humanity as a people. Perhaps we have to imagine first, or something larger—the wave of the collective imagina-tion—imagines us. We align ourselves with it.

As my beloved aunt spoke, I saw what a horse and rider could do when they aligned themselves of the same mind, and thirdly aligned themselves with the mind of the land. They were able to move with one body, one spirit, and the miraculous appeared to happen. It was possible; it is possible. I saw it all happen, all at once as

we drove through the land. She spoke carefully, was not elaborate or excessive in her talk. She simply constructed the backwards and forwards of time. We thought about it quietly as the road twisted and turned and we made our way through the late summer afternoon. Monahwee and his black horse crossed time and road along beside us. He was deserving of the horse blanket, as was his horse.

The world doesn't always happen in a linear manner. Nor does the existence of horses. Nature is much more creative than that, especially when it comes to time and the manipulation of time and space.

When the explorer Magellan traveled around the world by ship, he stopped at Tierra del Fuego. The indige-nous people who resided there could not see the huge flags of his ships as they docked out in the natural harbor. They had not previously imagined such structures and could not see them. (I'm sure, however, they saw the horses and knew they must keep some of these creatures for themselves.) Monahwee is on a horse and they are traveling toward us.

Monahwee has been written about often in history books dealing with Indian history, the history of southern Indians. He was a leader of the Battle of Horseshoe Bend, one of the largest Indian uprisings in the history of North America, an uprising against the travesty of injustice that had been set into place with the arrival of Christopher Columbus. The Battle of Horseshoe Bend was an armed conflict against Andrew Jackson and the U.S. govern-ment, against the forceful removal of our peoples from our homelands. This conflict rallied Creeks, Seminoles and associated Africans against this injustice. Monahwee suffered seven shot wounds, but survived by sheer force of will and love, for the people.

History also calls Monahwee a horse thief. He could capture horses easily and enjoyed making raids to acquire horses. What history doesn't say is that horses knew him, relished his smell, his manner. Monahwee didn't steal them, he didn't have to—they wanted to follow him and did, from the corrals of the European immigrants, from neighboring enemy tribes.

Once in my mid-twenties I was on a road trip between Albuquerque and Las Cruces. It was quiet except for the long howls of wind running through the canyons and the hum of the efficient motor of my small truck. Then a black horse appeared to me. First I smelled this horse of memory, appearing from the six generations back of Monahwee. In this smell was the hologram set off by the horse blanket acquired by my grandmother, the stories told me by my Aunt Lois. I was aware of a million details all at once, of this horse, of our old connection, of how we had once lived and died together, of my family's love of horses. We communed for several miles as tears ran down my face.

The power of horses continues to surround us. My cousin Donna Jo Harjo was a champion barrel racer, has the gift with horses that Monahwee demonstrated, and though she lives on a scant retirement check she has a beloved horse. My son's name, Phillip, is derived from an English word meaning "lover of horses." He is a natural horseman. Most recently we held a ceremony for my youngest granddaughter, Desiray Kiara Cheé. The horses appeared from the knowledge of the fire to surround her, as they continue to travel with the people in a manner that is beautiful.

"obsolete: not for navigational purposes"

Horsepower as a unit of measure is still the standard in the mechanical world. The horse, throughout time, has been integral to our efforts in agriculture, hunting, war, sports, and any laborious task that we have not been up to tackling. The indebtedness to these companions is deep.

My interest is in the history of art and western culture, and how human perceptions of these fields are formed.

Often the artwork that I make investigates our tendency to romanticize the past. And the horse is a perfect metaphor for this. The form of the horse, the dynamism of its movement in stride, is one of our very ideals of beauty. In these pieces I wanted to explore not just the surface appearance of the animal, but our relationship to it. The physiognomy of the horse is a symbol on which these designs are saddled.

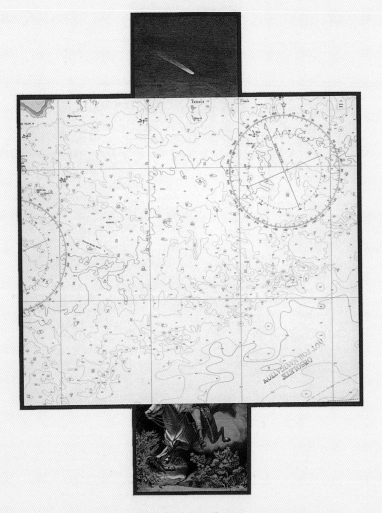

Land, Sea, and Air (collage on paper)

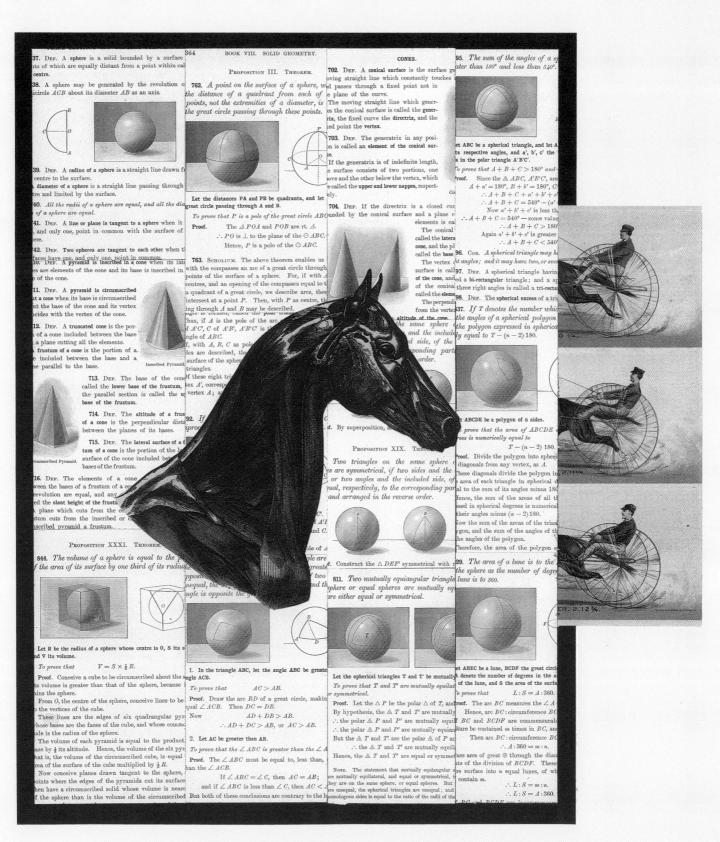

Evidence of Linear Progression (oil and collage on paper)

Black Obelisk (oil and collage on paper)

Run for the Roses (oil and collage on paper)

summer school

T. M. McNALLY

I learned to ride in Wisconsin, what some call God's country. It was the summer I was thirteen, and my father was recovering from a cerebral aneurysm, and I had prayed earnestly for him not to die. At the time he was forty-five, when the aneurysm, initially misdiagnosed as a migraine, had begun to leak. And my prayers were answered; my father did not die, though in order to save him the doctors felt compelled to perform, in addition to the then experimental surgery, a frontal lobotomy. It was a miracle, they said, congratulating themselves, and after seven months of rehab my father was still speechless; he arrived home in a long blue limo and could barely walk the few steps to our front door. My father, I soon learned, had also become epileptic, and that very day we left for Wisconsin, he had his first seizure at home.

Actually, it was in the garage. We had been loading up the car, one he had let me help pick out before his surgery as a birthday gift for my mother, who was now in the kitchen, packing, maybe talking on the phone to our priest, I don't recall . . . but I do remember my father, turning to me, as if asking for me to pass him the salt, or a wrench, and then his eyes clouded over and he fell on the concrete floor and began to writhe. It was all very violent. I remember calling for my mom and removing my wallet, which I had brought along special for our big trip to Wisconsin, and I remember placing my wallet in his mouth to prevent him from biting off his tongue. I remember his hands, thrashing against the side of the car, and the concrete. I remember that he was deeply ashamed, though he was of course unable to say anything about it. At the time he could still barely speak a word at all.

We went on our vacation, nonetheless, because my mother was feeling brave. We went to a dude ranch with GOLDEN PALOMINOS! on the sign in front of a long, winding driveway. The woman who owned the ranch was a widowed psychiatrist. She was also blind. I remember trying to buy cigarettes at the dude ranch convenience counter and disguising my voice, which the old blind shrink instantly recognized as belonging to the screwed-up kid with the crippled father and broken-hearted mother. I had wanted Marlboros, of course. For Cowboys. The blind woman told me smoking would stunt my growth and then kill me; thereafter my father bought the cigarettes, and we would sneak them together in the parking lot, avoiding fire hazards. It was a hot summer, worse at home, so we spent six weeks there, in Wisconsin, eating family-style meals. My mother could talk with the psychiatrist. My father, always at home with tools, could take walks and watch the maintenance workers repair the various pieces of broken machinery. And I could hang out with the wranglers in the barn.

It's odd, this comfort I feel with animals, and sometimes also with my father. I once heard a story about a retarded boy who could converse with horses. It's a fact I understand well: this ability to get on intuitively with our fellow creatures, especially those most comfortable with silence. I remember the blind woman explaining once to me the true nature of the relationship between rider and horse, drawing on a famous analogy that she said dated all the way back to Plato, whom of course I'd never heard of.

What she said was, The rider embodies Reason. And the horse? The horse supplies the Passion. And what connects the two are the reins and your knees.

Like I said, she was a psychiatrist, and though she'd never even *seen* a horse, she certainly had felt one: the size, the shape, the beating of its heart. She understood the need for balance, especially while climbing on; she understood the need to live tenderly among the spirits of this world. Meanwhile, I was thirteen, my father was now a ghost, and all of this, each and every part, is connected to who I am and what I have become.

For years I carried that wallet with me, and the tooth marks, bit into the leather.

We moved to Arizona, the Valley of the Sun.

There I grew up quickly, worked in stables and kennels, and left home to go to college far, far away. For two summers I ran a forty-horse stable for a girls camp in Minnesota. The summer I graduated from college, I was promoted to riding director for the boys camp across the lake. My job was to teach the camp counselors how to teach the kids to ride; my job was to keep everybody safe and happy during the summer of 1983.

I didn't know what I was going to do with my life once the summer was over. I had gone to college thinking I would grow up and become a rock star; then I read *The World According to Garp* (in the girls camp hay barn, the summer before) and decided that, given my lack of musical talent, I should probably become either an Episcopal priest or a novelist. Much of the construction of this dilemma had to do with my love for God and my desire to write books that people would read in barns or on buses and trains; I also believed mistakenly that the world was divided strictly into two halves, God's and ours, those same two halves described by the poet Edmund Spenser—earthly and heavenly. To be a priest was to serve my heavenly father. To be a writer, it seemed, was merely to serve myself.

Reason and Passion—the square root of paradox. Follow your heart, I was taught, but don't forget to use your head; pray to God, but always row for shore—this is what I was thinking about that summer. I should also point out that, for those so inclined anyway, it is very difficult to spend a lot of time around horses without also thinking a lot about God.

To begin with, they are big. They need you to be fully appreciated, though certainly they'd get on well enough without ever having been introduced to the descendants of either Cain or Abel. Also, and very much like God, a horse is capable of killing you within a heartbeat, though most of us would like to believe it would never do so on purpose. Anyone who's ever been kicked, or pinched in a stall, is well aware of the constant danger that comes with carelessness: it's hot, you're not paying attention, the horse is cranky at having been bitten at all day by flies the size of golf balls. And like God's, the vision of a horse is magnified. A dime, shining in the grass, can seem threatening as a truck, which is also to say, and unlike God, horses spook. And it is of course trucks and automobiles and jet fuel—the hard facts of modernity—that have made both God and horses increasingly irrelevant to our culture. What is lost is our respect and affection for—our connectedness to—our fellow creatures, as well as a divine admonition to care

for them properly. Imagine whispering something sweet to your automobile in traffic. Most people living today have never even touched a horse.

I've spent a lot of time thinking about it, the place of horses in our lives, which I think is what one does while shoveling a lot of shit. What goes in must come out: we'd go through thirty bales a day just for the mangers in the paddocks. An hour to clean the stalls, which we'd do mornings and afternoons. Another hour to sweep out the entire barn and spread the lime and spray for flies. Meanwhile I've shot horses full of medicine and trimmed their hooves and sewed up cuts from barbed-wire fences. We'd spread the manure in a field; the manure grew grass. Making hay, the world turned into one big metaphor, and while doing all of this wonderful manual labor, the kind of labor one does for a purpose, as opposed to wage, this care and feeding of all these beloved animals, I was mostly grateful for the opportunity to be so occupied. Everything, it seemed, was of use; everything absolutely mattered, especially the hay barn. That summer, in the evenings, I'd meet a girl I knew there, where the horses also had partial access: there we'd be (her name was Susan, and I loved her) all a-tousle, with Napoleon, after midnight, tugging on a bale beneath our feet. Or Cochise. Or Red Cloud. Mandingo. Silver Dollar. Bay Lady.

As riding director of a summer camp, one of my jobs was to name the new horses we'd buy from various traders. So when Harry Chapin died, I named a big old bay with smooth gaits Chapin. I named a horse Sanborn, after the saxophone player. As for my horse, the horse I rode, and kept to myself, and very nearly bought—his name was Sebastian: a name influenced by the saint, and the musician John Sebastian, as well as the character Sebastian Flyte from *Brideshead Revisited*, a man torn between, among other things, his love for God and the world.

Sebastian was a small, spirited sorrel with white socks and a particularly muscled neck and haunch, so what he lacked in size he made up for with endurance and strength. After a while he began to recognize my voice, and to understand that he was mine. My days would involve hours of ring work, teaching the nine-year-olds how to make friends and do a figure eight; the really advanced kids, most of whom rode often at home, would pass the day helping the little kids earn their Buckaroo badges; as a treat, the advanced riders would get to spend an hour or two whooping it up out in the huge pasture. During overnights we'd spend a lot of time trying to pick a Stetson up off the ground at a lope (a slow one). Mercifully, the ground was soft, and eventually I understood I wasn't teaching young men and women how to ride a horse. Rather I was teaching them how to be at peace with themselves. How to make the halves meet, between rider and horse, sensibility and heart.

First, you hold the reins, interlaced between two fingers, just so, because it only takes a flick of your wrist . . . you keep your heels down; you squeeze with your knees. Balance. Don't forget to breathe.

When Esmerelda died, I had to figure out what to do. She was old, older than the tractor, and then one day she just fell down, *dunk*. I knew she was dead from all the flies landing on her nose, and her eyes. My boss and I ended up dragging her from the paddock with a jeep. It was raining by then, and muddy; we covered her up with a tarp and kept her out of sight for two days until the knacker came by to pick her up. We hid her behind the old wagon with the rusty springs. The kids, especially the little ones, to whom she had spent the last five years of her life particularly dedicated, they all wanted to know what happened to Esmerelda. And naturally, I fibbed, explaining that The Headless Horseman had stolen her. The Headless Horseman was the evil demon who rode through the fields late at night, looking for his head, because of course he'd lost it.

It's important, I'd explain, to always keep your cool.

It was a good job. Thursdays we played Phil Donahue. This sweet kid with a big fouffy hairdo and thick glasses and knit shirts looked just like he belonged on television. So we'd stand him up on a barrel in the center of the ring, and he'd say, "Phil Donahue says trot your horses!"

The rules were the same as the game named after Simon, with losers having to dismount in the center. Years later I got a letter from the kid who told me that learning how to ride a horse was the best thing that ever happened to him. He signed it,

Your Friend, Phil Donahue.

Certainly my learning how to ride a horse was a blessing entirely undeserved. The lesson of Spenser's hymns to heaven and earth is that it is a sin to reject either, for both belong to us *and* to God. The meaning of paradox is that one needs both—reason and passion, gravity and flight, faith and uncertainty. God the father, God the son.

To ride a horse is to understand implicitly the laws of balance. Meanwhile, it feels like summer all over again, and my dogs are at my feet. I don't know what happened to Susan, though I do remember riding with her late at night, under the moon, amid all the loose horses in the field. She said later she always knew I'd go to graduate school in English. The thing about loving somebody is that it doesn't have to work out to save you from doing the wrong thing. Or the right thing. As for my father, he is better, but of course he is still a ghost. Prior to his illness, he had made his living in the automotive industry. There are patents in his name in countries all over the world. He, too, believes in horsepower, though it's not the kind of thing we've ever been able to talk about, given his difficulties with speech.

He has a grandson now, Theodore Harrison, born just last month. In the hospital, with my wife, breathing, the monitor hooked up, you could hear Teddy's tiny heartbeat galloping across the roof of her belly. Now, of course, I dream of teaching him to ride. I dream of finding him a safe place with a lot of land protected by the federal government nearby, and someday teaching him, this eight-year-old boy, or nine, this boy who weighs maybe sixty-five pounds, how to control with his hands and his heels a living creature big as a house, or school. I want to teach him how to care for it, and to name it, and to love it properly because this simply is his duty: to care for that which serves him and takes him places where he wants to go. I want to watch him learn to love—and not fear—that which is bigger than himself. I want to watch

him run his fingers through the mane.

In the summer of 1983, I'd wake at about six. I'd walk the half mile through the woods to the barn and start the coffee in the tack room. Then I'd bring the horses into the barn, already nickering for breakfast, nudging at the door. I'd bring them in five at a time, sorting them into their stalls, and then the saddling crew would come down, and after chores we'd sit around listening to Paul Harvey, drinking our coffee. Sometimes, when it rained, we'd just listen to that: the rain, pounding on the tin roof of the barn, and the horses, munching at their grain. We'd clean tack and tell stories and ask the kids to recite parts of the horse's body. On fair days, and there were lots of them that summer, we'd teach our classes, and maybe Susan and I would sneak a visit, in between Lunch and Rest Hour, and sometimes, when it was really hot, we'd chuck it all in and strip off the saddles and take the horses swimming in a lake. At the very end, each and every day, I'd unsaddle Sebastian and let him roll. Then I'd swing up, and we'd check the perimeter of the pasture, the fence—just me, my horse, and a hackamore. And when I think about this period in my life, my summer of wonder and delight, I think of the blue sky, and my horse, his spine digging into my body, and the way when you're on a horse with a fine gait, the world just opens up its doors to welcome you. It was this perfect moment, and I lived it often, and the sky was so clear I swear to God you could see halfway across the world.

horse and camera

I grew up riding ponies in the backyard with my two sisters, became a Ponyclubber, foxhunted, and rode in all of the local hunter shows. I spent a short time grooming in North Carolina, then came back to Minnesota to attend the university—still riding and grooming as my part-time job. During those "formative years" I picked up a still camera and have been intrigued ever since. Almost seven years ago I was offered my current horse job: training and showing Hanoverian horses that are owned, bred, and raised by a Canadian who lives in Medina. This farm is about a mile from where I grew up. Now, in addition to my camera work, I compete in Grand Prix jumping events with my horse William L.

Ciona

Des Surles

Jessy and Carly

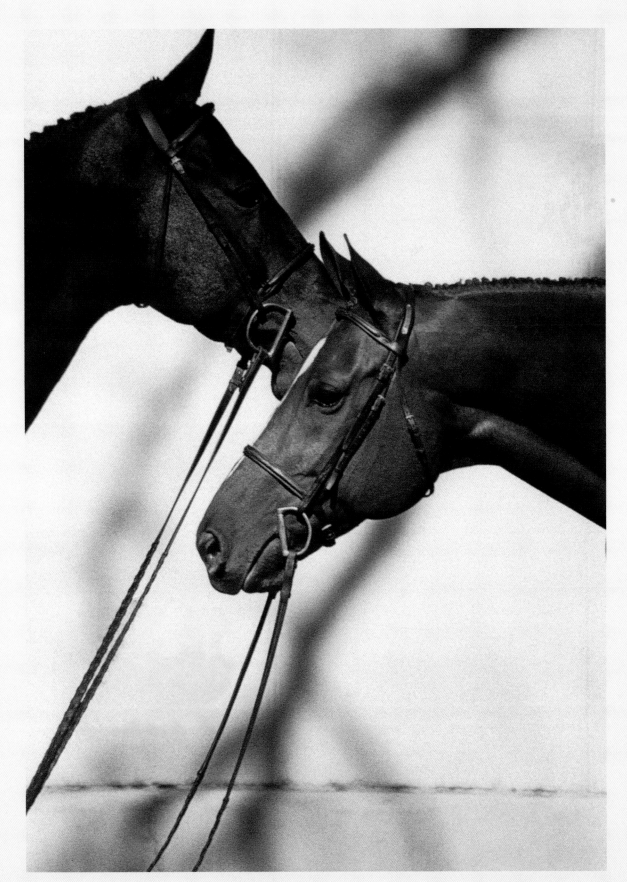

Tony and Bernie

On whitey

MICHELLE HUNEVEN

Fifteen years ago, I was living alone in the Southern Sierras on twenty-odd acres of fenced riverfront property when my friend Natalie called and offered to sell me Whitey, the twelve-year-old half-Arab, half-quarter-horse mare she'd rescued from a neighboring cattle ranch.

Real cowboys, at least real cowboys at that Sierran foothill ranch, did not ride white horses. Whitey had been kept for children and women to ride, and there weren't many of them at the ranch, especially after the rancher's wife took the kids and left. After their departure, the rancher told Natalie that Whitey was nothing but a hay burner now and he was going to "chicken her out." Thank God that Natalie, a horse breeder, not only understood the charming local idiom for butchering but

also couldn't bear the thought of it. She bought Whitey and reconditioned her—wormed her, fattened her up, called in the farrier, spent some time on her back sharpening Whitey's skills as a mount. When I came over for a visit, Natalie had me take Whitey for a spin. Whitey, it turned out, had only benefited from the cowboys' neglect: she was a fine riding horse, willing to please, polite, well-gaited, careful about where she put her feet. A few days later, when the quality of that ride had had a chance to sink in, Natalie phoned and offered Whitey to me for a very fair price.

Except for the times I galloped Christina Hernandez all over the playground pretending her long braids were reins, I had missed that stage in adolescence when a girl compulsively reads *Black Beauty* and *Misty of Chincoteague* and thinks mucking stables the apex of privilege. I didn't start riding until I was nineteen, and while I liked and admired horses, I had no particular skill or rapport with them, and never acquired the expertise that comes effortlessly with devout interest. By the time Natalie offered me Whitey, I had already owned one horse, a quarter-horse cow pony named Ramon, who shortly after I bought him kicked up a strand of barbed wire, panicked, and threw me in such a way I compressed and fractured several vertebrae and, once I was allowed out of bed, had to wear a metal back brace for three months. (When I was in the hospital, I learned Ramon had a history of panicking: He'd sent a previous owner to the hospital after stepping in four inches of mud.)

I didn't hold Ramon's bad moments against horses in general, however, and continued to ride when the opportunity arose. I still liked horses, and Whitey in particular seemed sweet. Also, living alone and having fenced acreage made me extremely vulnerable to renewed horse ownership. But mostly, a resurgent interest in horses had been piqued by a curious book I found at a rummage sale by the Nobel Prize-winning Belgian playwright Maurice Maeterlinck in which there was a long essay on the Elberfield horses.

Most people have heard of Clever Hans, the horse in Germany who was said to perform feats of mathematical wizardry and to communicate with humans in spelled-out words. A stern, unkind old eccentric named Wilhelm von Osten had taught Hans first to count, then to read, then to listen discerningly to music—it was said that Hans could distinguish between harmonious and discordant chords and, all told, that he had the intellectual capabili-

ties of an intelligent fourteen-year-old schoolboy. Hans and his owner were quickly discredited. In fact, Clever Hans became known as one of the great frauds of the twentieth century. The scientist who discredited him said that the horse was not actually doing the mental calculations, but was responding to "imperceptible, infinitesimal and unconscious signals from its master."

The discreditor's reasoning stopped me short in my reading: So what if Hans couldn't calculate the square root of 9,632—I couldn't, either. The fact that Hans could respond to such subtle signals seemed extraordinary enough. What, I wondered, would an unconscious signal be? And how could you train a horse to decipher it?

According to Maeterlinck, von Osten died humiliated and embittered—yet he did have a disciple to carry on his work, one Herr Krall, a wealthy manufacturer who inherited Clever Hans and also acquired other horses of his own, Muhamed and Zarif, whom he trained in his spare time. In two short weeks of training, Muhamed was doing simple additions and subtractions, and four days after that he began multiplication and division.

Maeterlinck himself visited Elberfield, where he saw old Hans, now out to pasture having severely injured—really, ruined—himself trying to leap out of his stall to get to a mare. Maeterlinck was also able to observe Muhamed and Zarif perform their remarkable calculations. He was left alone with the horses, and asked them mathematical questions whose answers he himself didn't know; the horses responded with convincing accuracy. Ultimately, Maeterlinck credited neither the horses' intellectual capabilities nor human trickery, but a grander universal and mystical intelligence that horses apparently are able to access. The problem and the solution to a problem exist simultaneously, Maeterlinck believed, and horses, or these horses, hearing of one, immediately knew the other.

Whatever the explanation—tremendous intellectual capacity, the ability to receive and respond to the subtlest of messages, and/or a mystic's access to universal facts—horses and their intelligence seemed one of the world's most alluring mysteries. And owning Whitey became a way to investigate it for myself. Having no idea how to begin to tap such intelligence, I asked Natalie how she trained her Morgans to do such generic horse activities as dressage. "Each step of the way," she said, "I have to reach deep into a horse's psyche"—here, she made a gesture as if reaching into a high, deep cookie jar—"find just the right connection, and make an adjustment." Her hand turned an invisible faucet.

The day after Whitey came to live at my place, I saddled her and climbed on board. Looking down at her big sweet head, I thought, how does one reach inside there, gain access to that wiring, locate a level of response? Whitey's roached mane and long, white bangs offered no clue.

We sauntered down the dirt drive. I patted Whitey's flank, murmured encouragement. Sleek, well-fed, she walked calmly, avoiding ruts and rocks with a pleasing precision. As we went through the gate and out onto the road, she was alert and responsive and altogether tractable. She was, I thought, as pleased to be with me as I was to be with her.

But when we came to the Tule River Bridge, she would not cross. Even where the asphalt road was just turning into a bridge with guardrails on the sides and solid ground below, Whitey would step no further. I gave

her a little kick with my heels. She went sideways. I turned her around, walked her a few paces off, brought her round again to the bridge. No go. I dismounted, walked on the bridge myself, spoke soothingly, tried leading her across. Nix. I tried pulling her and she actually reared, albeit timidly and not very high. This was ridiculous. Surely she'd crossed countless bridges in her decade as a kid's saddle horse. I gazed into her bottomless, long-lashed Arabian sloe eyes. Was she genuinely frightened, or testing me? Or was it sheer stubbornness and she simply preferred not to cross? She returned my gaze with no discernible expression. What could I do or say to reach deep down into that equine psyche and change Whitey's mind about bridges?

Three days later, we still had not crossed the river.

I called Natalie. "Whitey won't cross the Tule River Bridge," I said, and told her everything I'd tried.

"I have only one thing to say to you," said Natalie. "Are you listening?"

"Yes."

"Whitey hates pain."

"But I haven't hurt her," I cried. "Not even a little!"

"And therein lies your problem," said Natalie.

I cut a nice, springy willow switch. One with a good little sting to it. I showed this switch to Whitey before I got on her back, and again when I was mounted, so the mere sight of it wouldn't give her a jolt. I then kept the switch out of sight until we got to the bridge. She started in with her won't-brook-the-bridge routine with absolute confidence. She shied, executed some fancy sidestepping. Stood stock still.

I signaled with a tap of my heels, landed one sharp, stinging snap on her snowy rump and clucked. A tremor ran the length of Whitey's back, and with no more ado we were on the bridge. Walking. I would have to say our pace was stately.

Below us, the saddle-brown water was fringed with greening willows: surely there were enough switches on those banks to make Whitey learn spelling and counterpoint in music, not to mention algebra, geometry, and calculus.

After that initial impasse, I never used a switch on her again. And she never did become a Clever Hans. Over time, however, as we galloped on old fire roads and followed deer paths deep into the woods, Whitey revealed herself to me. She was, it turned out, not only willing and careful but, once she settled in, unusually friendly—almost like a dog in her affections. Every time I came out of the house with her bridle, she sauntered up to meet me. Most of the time I rode her with only a halter. Such compliance alone seemed miraculous, and never failed to give me pleasure. In one lingering image, I see us going down a steep slope densely littered with loose, oblong rocks. (On Ramon, this would have been a sure ticket to the hospital.) I gave her lots of rein and leaned back, observing how, with startling precision, she meticulously and unerringly located and placed each foot on solid ground.

I left her behind with a friend when I moved back to the city and she died not long afterwards. As I remember Whitey, though, she is healthy, sound and, in her own fashion, both clever and curious. She learned to lift the hasp on my gate with her whiskery muzzle and, if I'd left the door ajar for the dogs, she'd nudge it open and slip inside. More than once I'd be in my house reading or working at my desk when I'd hear a noise that sounded as if the heavy furniture had come to life and was stumbling through the house. And there she'd be, a suddenly huge, dappled white horse standing between the sofa and the woodstove, hooves planted in the carpet, ears pricked, her big dark eyes calmly inspecting my living quarters.

DEBORAH BUTTERFIELD

work horses

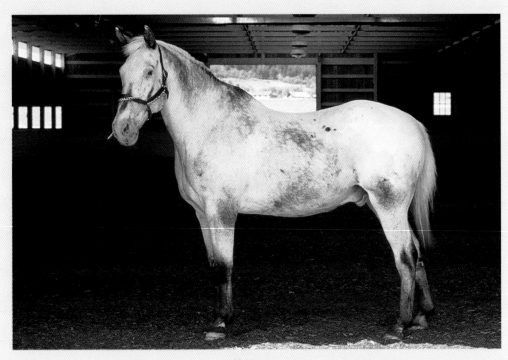

Hoover

Hoover, 1984 (found steel)

Punch, 1997 (cast bronze)

Argus (PJ), 1997 (cast bronze)

Willy, 1997 (cast bronze)

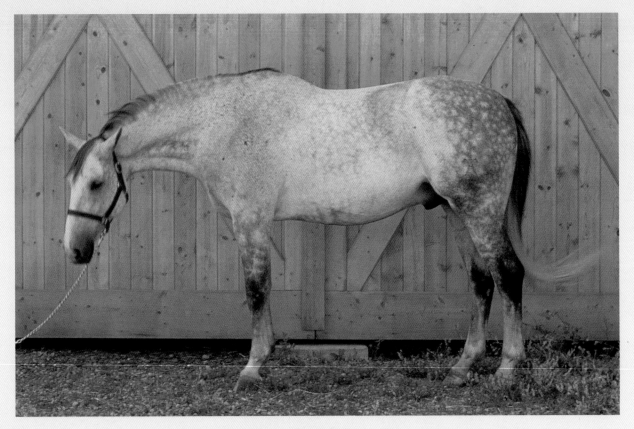

Ismani

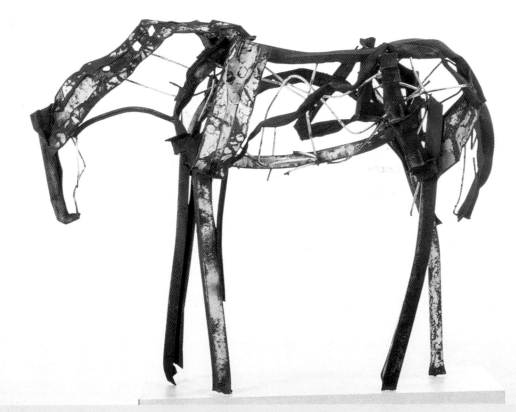

Ismani, 1995 (found steel)

good horSe keeping

PAUL ZARZYSKI

Life is a catch pen full of rodeo broncs, and the way I figure it, forty-six years into this buck-out, the mission is to decide, early on, *Did you come to hide or did you come to ride?* If the latter, it doesn't take too many seasons forked to this buckin' horse orb named Earth before we learn the crude rude truth of the old adage: *Never a pony couldn't be rode, never a cowboy couldn't be throwed.* And subordinating this proverb is yet another cowpoke dictum: *Get pitched off, climb right back on.* Rodeo, like Poetry, can get into your hemoglobin, into the deep helices of DNA, and once there, it becomes your metaphorical makeup for life.

In Spanish, *rodear* means "to surround"; in colloquial Mexican, it means "a cattle roundup." *A-horseback* is understood, and understood so emphatically, that only bull riders (I can *cow*-poke fun at them here because most can't read anyway) might disagree that rodeo *means* horses. Moreover, I think rodeo cowboys relate to horses in ways that very well could qualify them as the staunchest of animal rights advocates. But let's put the raucous Yosemite Sam WHOA! on opening that Pandora's Saddlebag right now and lope off instead toward a few poems that have graced my Lariati-Literati Life because, I choose to believe, my Muse has some Annie Oakley, Mr. Ed, Saint Francis of Assisi, Midnight, and My Friend Flicka in her bloodlines.

In the days when rodeo fever popped the cork and geysered the mercury out of my genuine Hopalong Cassidy bucking bronco thermometer, all I thought about was horses, Horses, HORSES! My focus burned so intensely that I became unable to discern the word *house* in print, which made for some interesting magazines at the newsstand. You had your *Horse Beautiful*, your *Good*

Horse Keeping, your *Horse and Garden*. Same syndrome occurred with the word radio: National Public Rodeo, Rodeo Free Europe, Rodeo City Music Hall, and that little kid's wagon called a Rodeo Flyer. In any case, I'd be driving all night between rodeos and listening to the rodeo—I mean radio—to stay awake, and I'd look up at that full moon, and its Rorschach test shadow always appeared to me as the image of a bronc rider sittin' pretty in his leather throne on a high-rollin' bucker. Years later, I wrote this "rodeo romance."

THE BUCKING HORSE MOON

A kiss for luck, then we'd let 'er buck—
I'd spur electric on adrenaline and lust.
　She'd figure-8 those barrels
on her Crimson Missile sorrel—
　　we'd make the night air swirl with hair and dust.

　At some sagebrushed wayside, 3 A.M.,
we'd water, grain, and ground-tie Missile.
　Zip our sleeping bags together,
make love in any weather,
　　amid the cactus, rattlers, and thistle.

　Seems the moon was always full for us—
it's high-diving shadow kicking hard.
　We'd play kid games on the big night sky,
she'd say "that bronco's Blue-Tail Fly,
　　and ain't that ol' J. T. spurrin' off its stars?"

　We knew sweet youth's no easy keeper.
It's spent like winnings, all too soon.
　So we'd revel every minute

in the music of our Buick
　running smooth, two rodeoin' lovers
cruising to another—
　beneath Montana's blue roan
bucking horse moon.

　The Augusta show at 2, we'd place again,
then sneak off to our secret Dearborn River spot.
　We'd take some chips and beer and cheese,
skinny-dip, dry off in the breeze,
　　build a fire, fry the trout we caught.

　Down moonlit gravel back to blacktop,
she'd laugh and kill those beams for fun.
　That old wagon road was ours to own—
30 shows since I'd been thrown
　　and 87 barrels since she'd tipped one.

　We knew that youth won't keep for rainy days.
It burns and turns to ash too soon.
　So we'd revel every minute
in the music of our Buick
　running smooth, two rodeoin' lovers
cruising to another—
　beneath Montana's blue roan
bucking horse moon.

Ahhh, "sweet youth"—and no, it's truly not an "easy keeper" (said of a horse who winters well, holding his weight on minimal feed). And though the equine species, from sixty-million-year-old eohippus (the prehistoric "dawn horse," no bigger than a cocker spaniel) to today's mustangs, has drunk out of a lot more watering holes than we Homo sapiens, they haven't discovered the fountain of youth, either. Depending on vocation, a horse is usually considered to have reached retirement age at anywhere from six to eight years (racehorses) to twelve to fifteen years (roping, reining, show horses) to eighteen to twenty-two years (ranch/stock horses). On the average, horses age approximately three years for every human year. By the time they're twenty or twenty-two, they're often referred to as "pensioners" and put out to pasture just like us two-legged folks. If there *were* an Adam and Eve, and if they *were* responsible (having bitten into that measly McIntosh) for the injustices and disparities of today's world, I especially hold against them the so-called fact of life wherein the most common four-legged members of our families—dogs, cats, horses, rabbits, etc.—enjoy only a fraction of our longevity. It ain't my fault; I don't even like apples that much, and usually wind up feeding them out of the fruit bowl to our twenty-three-year-old mare, Cody (her favorite treat, next to getting into the bird feeder).Therefore should I ever be designated Creator for a Day, one of my first duties will be to see to it that horses live as long as parrots or turtles.

Speaking of religion, of the miracle of life, of that glowing, glowering coal of youth that stays a-smolder and waiting, in most of us I hope, for a stiff wind to blow away the soot and ash and expose the fire, I watched Big George Foreman—who trained like a Clydesdale as he harnessed himself to a jeep and pulled it around his neighborhood—convincingly win a fight recently against a very strong thirty-two-year-old opponent. George is forty-eight. At the Red Lodge Rodeo years ago, I saw a black mare named High Prairie buck off the World Champion Saddle Bronc Rider and do a little soft shoe in the middle of him to add just a skosh of injury to the incredible insult. In the midst of a couple dozen cowboys straining to restrain their chuckles in back of the bucking chutes, I swear I heard old High Prairie nickering all the way back to the catchpen: ". . . never a cowboy couldn't be throwed, be throwed, be throwed." I *know* Sonny and Pat Linger, High Prairie's guardians, heard her because they made no effort at all to curb their knee-slappin' delight. By the way, that horse was thirty-three years old at the time. I wonder if Big George will still be climbing into the ring at ninety-nine?

I wish my saddle horse, Buck (short for Buckskin, actually), could have lived into his George Years (Foreman, Burns) as High Prairie lived so vibrantly into hers. The morning I found him dead in the corral, I phoned the neighbor—hoping to borrow his tractor—and when, in relating my situation, I choked up and broke down, he responded, "It's just a horse." Understand that he's not a cruel man; unlike myself, who didn't begin hanging around horses day-to-day until my twenties, he'd likely been aboard them since he was three or four; his family had owned dozens, bought and sold them, watched them come and go, live and die. Although I had come to know "intimately" hundreds of rodeo broncs, Buck was sort of my first, shall we say, partner. I don't know if my good friend and neighbor ever sat in front of the TV at midnight while eating a bowl of Wheaties, mid-January Montana windchill temps pushing eighty below zero, and thought to himself, "Wonder if my horse is craving a late-night snack, too," then bundled up in umpteen layers and plodded, like a moon-walking astronaut, to serve up a half canful of grain and a couple alfalfa flakes?

Maybe he has. And maybe he's missed his lost horses as much as I've missed mine and grieved every bit as hard.

BUCK

The December my horse died, I did not
go to midnight mass
to celebrate with a single sip of wine
Christ's birth. Instead, lit

between a nimbus moon and new snow,
I guzzled mescal and mimicked the caroling
coyotes down the crick

where weeks earlier I dragged Buck
behind the pickup—horizontal
hooves at an awkward trot

in the side mirror, an image
I'll take with me to hell. No backhoe,
no D-8 Cat to dig a grave with, I left

him in deep bunchgrass, saffron
belly toward the south
like a warm porch light thrown

suddenly over those singing
Nó-el, No-el . . .
            Riding the same ground

that past spring for horned cow skulls
to adorn our gates, I spotted four
bleached white as puffballs,

methodically stuffed them
into a never-tear trash bag,
balanced the booty

off one thigh and tried to hold
jog-trot Buck to a walk,

my forefinger hefting
the left rein to curb
his starboard glance.

                One by one,
like spook-show aliens hatching
from human brisket, white shoots popped

through that hot black plastic
gleaming in noon sun that turned
my grasp to butterfat. And when I reached,

lifting to retwist my grip,
it was sputnik flying low, it was
Satan's own crustacean unleashed, it was the

prehistoric, eight-horned, horse-eating bug
that caught Buck's eye
the instant his lit fuse hit powder. Lord,

how that old fat pony, living
up to his name one last time,
flashed his navel at angels,

rattled and rolled my skulls like dice,
and left me on all fours
as he did on that Christmas—high-

lonesomed, hurt, and howling
not one holy word toward the bones.

I never again road east—toward Buck's bones. By now, I suppose someone could have picked up his skull and hung it on their gate or barn. I guess that thought bothers this former grave-robber a bit. Most ranches have established boneyards to which winter-killed stock is dragged for decades and decades. Renowned western writer Teresa Jordan offers a passage in *Riding the White Horse*

Home about the critical moment in which a horseman works a colt toward the bones. The idea is to slowly and gently expose the young animal to everything and anything that might later, under sudden first-time encounters, instinctively cause him to spook. Whether they recognize it as such or not, horses do not like the look, or smell, of death. Ol' Buck illustrated this to me in no uncertain terms. I suppose most herbivores feel the same way.

The spring following Buck's departure, our mare, Cody, foaled on Memorial Day. I was in my rodeo-old forties—my riggin'-riding days pretty much history—and was struggling with resigning myself to a life between youth and death, complete with the reentry of the words *house* and *radio* into my old geezer language. I was missing then, and likely will forever miss, the challenge of, and the elation after, making a classy ride on a snappy bronc. I was also missing my rodeo *compadres;* the majority of them had, years back, begun to take on normal lives—marriages, mortgages, steady jobs, children—but the truth be known, I missed those bucking horses most, their personalities and temperaments far more akin to my own than that of fellow humans with whom I cross trails these days.

ᴄᴍᴏ

One of the premier horse gentlers in the West, Randy Rieman, who I have the honor of calling friend, is riding colts full-time for the Parker Ranch in Hawaii. He encounters very few horses that he can't coach toward feeling safe, at ease, and maybe even "fulfilled" with saddle and cowboy aboard. Randy told me recently,

however, of one three-year-old, after days and days of groundwork, that bucked, under his first saddling, from 5 P.M. till sundown. A horse like that will probably wind up in a rodeo string and have a good long career of eight-second workdays, according to Randy. "My kind of guy," I thought, and kept the notion to myself, knowing how important it is to Randy to find—to watch and listen and feel for—whatever unique equine code and/or communication will convince each individual horse to place his trust in the funny-lookin' critter standing upright.

So Cody gave birth to a healthy filly we named Rosebud—not Rodeo Rose or Widow Maker, Whiplash or Reller's Wreck, Snake Eyes, Aces-'n'-Eights, Sky Lab, Booger Red, Crash, Moonshine, or Midnight. And although it *was* Memorial Day, I felt no cemetery visitation obligation: Ol' Buck had not received a formal burial or headstone. Few horses do. One of the greatest rodeo champions of all time, however, not only has a marble, but one engraved with verse. I stood before his final resting place recently at The National Cowboy Hall of Fame in Oklahoma City and felt something powerful in both the place and the words—

> *Underneath this sod lies a great*
> *bucking hoss*
> *There never lived a cowboy he*
> *couldn't toss*
> *His name was Midnight, his coat*
> *black as coal*
> *If there's a horse heaven, please, God,*
> *rest his soul.*

—and what I felt somehow reflected off the poem I wrote that Memorial Day in praise to parturition, equine-style:

I AM NOT A COWBOY

because cowboys don't cry and I can't fight back
my 4-H'er greenhorn rapture
while watching Cody foal—no white socks up front,
a blazed face breaking through the giant dew-
drop into the 10:15 A.M. sun,
two hind socks stretched side-by-side in the dirt
like reverse white-on-black exclamation marks, and
yup it's a filly! Because real cowboys frown
unless it's a horse colt with four black feet,
this poem, I suppose, should tone down
its jubilation. Sorry fellers, for losing it,
but this cute little filly finds her footing
fast as you can think that single big syllable
HEART. And she stays up, pivoting
off mom's legs, like a ring-wise prize
fighter using the corner posts and ropes,
to gather herself after taking
birth's hard shot. It's Memorial Day
but these tears are not for the fallen
because I'm out here cheering on new life,
no taps bugled sad in the breeze
through these balm-of-Gileads
as the suckling foal's curled upper lip
blossoms, her gums
the pink-red rosebud-persimmon
color I think of when I think of the living,
when I think, again, of HEART. Let's rhyme it,

for tradition's sake, with smart.
Let's make this poem cowboy and make up some
for the poet, who tries but just can't quite
swallow hard enough his joy
as four more quarter horse quarter note
hooves step their first
Rosebud-with-Cody
sorrel stroll around our corral.

> *—For Elizabeth*

Cody and Rosebud now make up one half of our quarter-horse quartet, which we consider the most interesting, in many ways, two thirds of our family of six. When we left the large ranch where Buck died and Rosebud was born, we had a hard time finding an affordable place with enough acreage on which to keep our four horse people. Folks close to our predicament admonished, "Why not sell them?" To which we sometimes replied, "For the same reasons, we suppose, you haven't opted as yet to sell Jimmy or Suzy." In my opinion there are few differences. Sure, it costs a little more to keep our horses in shoes and food, and their schooling doesn't come cheap, either—not to even mention vet bills and worming medicine. On the other hand, we didn't have to invest a single frustrating day in potty training. There is, however, one extremely significant and difficult difference: unlike guardians of sons and daughters, we've had to come to accept, and even hope, that our horses will die before us. Only then can we ensure that their entire lives are lived with the most humane care a "people person" can offer a "horse person." On second thought, maybe God—Her Pegasus Paint Self—got it right after all?

red bandanna

horSes crOss, donkEys croSs

JANE HIRSHFIELD

In my mid-thirties, I came across a diary I had kept when I was ten—my first and last experiment with journal-keeping. It was a small, leather-bound volume, complete with padlock and tiny key. The edges of the paper were dyed gold, as was the stamping on the white cover: "My Diary." What struck me immediately as I turned its pages was how little my interests had changed. Boys, poetry, the family dog, the state of the petunias I grew on my bedroom's windowsill, spiritual probing, friends—and horses. By ten, it seems, I was set on my path, and though another decade has passed since I reencountered that young self, my passions and interests continue to run along those early-established lines. Perhaps, like a stream digging steadily more deeply the gully it runs in, it is a matter of presence increasing presence: what you are interested in grows ever more interesting.

It is not that nothing has changed. "Boys" became one steady life partner, those New York City apartment petunias have proliferated into a garden with a dozen fruit trees, a plot of vegetables, and a brace of old roses, irises, foxgloves, penstemon, and lilies. My current dog, a border collie, is entering her early, affectionate dotage, sufficiently deaf to no longer fear thunder or the wall heater's rattle. The child who once said to her mother, "It's too bad we're not Catholic—I can't become a nun" eventually spent years in strict monastic life, studying

Zen; and the friendships and poems have similarly found their own more ripened nature. As for the horses, that child's excitement at taking the big palomino Stonewall (I have since met others who remember him fondly, among them the Expressionist painter Paul Brach, twenty years my senior) from the rental stable on West 89th Street across traffic-filled avenues to the dirt paths of Central Park has never faded. There was, though, a not-uncommon gap: from fourteen to twenty-nine, my life was for the most part unhorsed.

Then, while sleeping one August morning in a meadow in California's High Sierra, my then boyfriend and I were wakened by a small group of passing riders. "That one," he called, from inside our zipped-together down bags. "She for sale?" She was a nameless bay, nine or ten years old, a ranch horse who we learned later had probably spent time on the fairgrounds track circuit. The next time we walked out of the high country for groceries, we returned leading the mare and her packsaddle with its dented metal boxes, an English saddle for riding out from base camp tied on the top. During the walk, we settled on Tainara for a name, though I lobbied hard for Jameson's, for the unwatered-whiskey color of her coat.

I am amazed now how well it all worked out. We learned that a little whipping cream carried fourteen miles over a ten-thousand-foot blue-granite pass is perfectly thickened for Irish coffee by nightfall. A horse in need of a treat will enjoy a slightly over-the-hill zucchini. One in hobbles can't canter quite far enough without tiring to actually get away, and hobbles are better than a rope left long for grazing; wrapped into its tangle, she stood calmly while I pressed down her nose to release the halter buckle's tension, then unwound her back legs.

Tainara was wise and steady and took good care of her two new owners, who had no idea how poor an idea it is to take a strange horse alone into the mountains over difficult trails, assuming her shoes would stay on, assuming no injury or panic too serious would come her way. And she, and we, were lucky—none did. After another six weeks we came down for the last time that summer, and trailered her to the pasture where she would stay for the next eight years, most of them retired with navicular disease from those early years of hard running. Or so the vet and farrier guessed—she had already been nerved once for pain relief, the vet found, and at the time it was thought too risky to try it again.

Then came seven years of sponsoring one horse, three years of another. When the second was offered to me for my own, the vet who checked him said, "You may have six years, you may have six months." Six months almost to the day after I took him, he started to show some unevenness at the trot, and a few months later I decided to retire him, given the steepness of the trails we traveled and the fact that every half year or so I seemed to find myself on the ground instead of his back—in a tight spot, he was a horse who would always get through, but a glimpse of a mouse, a leaf, or plume of pampas grass in an unexpected spot, and he was gone . . .

Still, Galahad—an Arab-Standardbred cross who had done fifty-mile endurance rides with his previous owners—made a *serious* rider of me, and now I seem to be trying to return the favor. My new companion is a six-year-old Arab, Flame, who knew less of the world than I realized when we were introduced. But how can you resist a horse who whinnies at you when you walk away after your first test ride? "Did you teach him to do that?" I asked the woman.

"I'd be a rich trainer if I could do that," she answered.

I tracked down what I could of Flame's history, and there wasn't much: a greatly admired grandfather, Bey Shah; a total of six months' training here and there. But his greenness had its good side: this, I knew, was a horse who hadn't already been worked overly hard, one who might travel with me for more than a few years. So together we are learning what we need to know to navigate wooden bridges, cliffside trails that slicken with ocean fog in winter, streams that need fording. To learn also how to carry the head low and relaxed, to walk uphill with energy and drive, to stay calm when another horse canters away. Flame is my first experience of riding a horse who hasn't already found the good trust that can carry a horse and rider through, who doesn't yet know his own confident strength for the task at hand; my first experience, too, of riding a horse with a good and kind eye, but also a temper. And so I find myself reading the new philosophers of horse-training, Ray Hunt and Tom Dorrance, with as much intensity and curiosity as I ever brought to discovering how a poem by Keats or Hopkins moves and sings.

What I, and others I've talked to, have found about growing older is this: Everything connects. Parts of a life you think you walked away from suddenly return—a high school friend, a companion in Zen training, and a fellow poet stand together at a reading reception, comparing notes; an experiment for a grade-school science class carries seed into runner beans' scarlet blossoms decades later. I've begun to see how a whole life goes into building a friendship with a young horse: knowing the sixteenth-century Zen painter Hakuin's saying, "The zafu [meditation cushion] and the saddle are the same"; the long tasting of the subtle rhythms of words; the slow-won realization that a poet who will not risk the unfamiliar is a poet who will not discover the thought unsuspected but already resident within; and that a horse unasked cannot even attempt the new task.

And what I learn now with Flame informs the rest of my life as well: here is a being who requires of me a consistent presence, an even-mindedness without anger, an encouraging spirit even when I myself am also nervous. Who requires of me the judgment to know when to ask more, when to loosen the reins, when to get off and hand-walk him past the troublesome moment. An ear flicked back at my shifting weight means I must recognize that every act between us is an act of communication. A tail switch informs me if I have requested something too harshly, a head shake or buck of frustration announces I have asked simply too much.

In one Zen koan, a monk comes to visit the great teacher Joshu, who inquires by what route he came. "From the south," the monk replies. Joshu then asks, "Did you cross my magnificent stone bridge?" "I saw no such bridge," the monk answers. The master can only respond sadly: "Horses cross, donkeys cross."

Though still a practitioner of Zen, I now live a fully ordinary-looking household life. Flame, though, lives in a pasture on Buddhist fields, at the practice community of Green Gulch in Muir Beach. Like any Zen master, he eats when he is hungry, sleeps when tired—except when I come to take him from that ease and ask him to travel some distance out of his moment-by-moment expression of true horse-nature to meet me in mine. That he will do this with me is pure gift; that a being not human will come with good cheer into our realm and allow us to come into his has not, in all these decades, ceased to move and thrill me.

When I first fell in love with horses I did not want to ride them, I simply wanted to be one. That I cannot have. But when I think, "Head long and low," and see the neck begin to stretch out, and feel the legs follow, the stride lengthen, a joy begins in me that includes not only horse but also the wild hill grasses, the fragrant sage and wind-bent lupine, the circling red-tailed hawk.

Perhaps the thread that stitches together all my early and continuing passions is the thread of connection, of seeking ways to participate in a wider life: with other humans, with other species, with other existence. Two fundamental teachings of Buddhism are transience and interconnection—and though horse and hawk and wildflowers and I will each of us vanish like blown seeds of dandelion, the connection between us and its continuance is equally a truth of the heart. And though it may be foolish to think so, I like to believe my joy is shared, to believe that the red ear swivels back to me not only in a prey animal's constant attentiveness but also in the pleasure two vastly different herd animals can take in their meeting.

The bridge we are currently working on is made of gray cedar that grows slippery with invisible mosses in winter. Flame treats it with appropriate caution. Still, horses cross, donkeys cross. People cross as well, sometimes walking and cajoling, sometimes riding in the company of one who teaches how to live in the scent and flare of this moment, who knows what it is to be a connected self.

JOHN DERRYBERRY

kashmir

the bluebird of happiness

GRETEL EHRLICH

I bought Blue from a Mormon horse trader in 1978 for $400. "He's worth a little more than the others because he's got some cow in him," the trader told me. Meaning, he liked to work cattle. "He probably knows a little more about cowboying than you do and that's good. You'll learn something from him if you keep your ears up." The trader supplied all the horses for the sheepherders on the 200,000-acre ranch where I had lived for two years.

Sheepherder horses are rarely things of beauty. They're usually old, hairy-legged, often white (an unpopular and impractical color). In other words, the horses, like the herders who rode them, were the unwanted ones in society.

Blue was long-headed, donkey-eared, hairy-legged, and had spots. He had been sired by a Government Remount stallion—now a thing of the past. These stud horses were taken around small communities and for a very nominal sum would breed a rancher's mares. It was the fast and economical way of increasing one's horse herd. The stallions were part of the original quarter-horse breed—big, stout, drafty, with just enough thoroughbred to get them moving and turning fast. And they had plenty of "cow." Which is why Blue looked the way he did and loved to sort cattle.

He arrived at the end of a very bad winter. I had suffered the loss of my fiancé and had been living alone in a one-room log cabin on a road out of Cody, Wyoming, that wasn't always plowed. As soon as the snow melted and the winglike drifts gripping my house began to melt,

Dave Cozzens arrived with Blue in the back of his red stock truck. There was no ramp or loading dock so Dave just jumped him out of the back. "He's a damned practical horse, if nothing else," he said.

We turned him out into a large pasture. The first night he was lonely so I sat on the fence in my long flannel nightgown and held his head in my arms until he quieted down. We were both bereaved and he was salve to my wounded mind.

When spring came I moved across the Big Horn Basin to a little town in the foothills of the Big Horn Mountains. The log house was bigger and Blue's pasture was luxuriant with early grass and a fast-running creek moving through. I rode him to the post office, then back the other way, past the pink house and the petroglyphs into the bug-ridden meadows that smelled of wild mint. Looking up, I could see the sunlit rock walls of a long canyon that cut all the way to the mountaintop.

That same week, an extraordinary woman, "Mike" Tisdale Hinckley, asked me to go cowboying with her. "I'll be there at 5 A.M. and you can take those damn sheepherder's pots and pans off your saddle," she said. Sheepherders are the brunt of everyone's jokes. When I loaded Blue into the trailer beside Mike's fancy quarter horse, we began laughing. "God, I should have come when it was still dark, so no one could see what I was hauling," she said. That summer we gathered and trailed cattle in the Big Horns and the Wolf Mountains in Montana. Everyone laughed at Blue—but that was an asset. When I laughed just as hard, everyone knew that at least I had a sense of humor—the first prerequisite on any ranch.

Blue was eight years old when I bought him. He was hard-mouthed and head-shy. He'd been beaten and abused and could be difficult. Once he almost dragged my friend Laura to death. She'd gotten a rope wrapped around her thigh and he spooked, not knowing she was attached to the line. Eventually he stopped and she survived—she had a lot of cuts and bruises, which I cleaned, nothing else.

On his good side, Blue traveled farther than any other horse and stayed at it for more hours. At the end of a fifty-mile circle gathering cattle, he still had enough juice to sort strays out of the herd and pair up mother cows and calves. All I had to do was let the reins loose and touch his withers. He'd do the rest.

Every year I rode hard all summer and fall, and when the snow flew Blue was turned out with the other horses until spring. In March or April I'd catch him, hold his big mule ears, and make my annual pact: "Are we going to get along this year, you old lunkhead, or am I going to have to sell you to the canners?" I'd ask sweetly. I could almost see him smile. Then he'd put in another seven or eight hundred miles, carrying me.

Sometimes in the autumn, when the ranch work slowed down, we'd take idyllic rides up into the mountains. I'd always let Blue pick his own trail. He loved to smell trees, bushes, and flowers. At eight thousand feet he'd stick his nose into the powdery yellow pollen flying off lodgepole pines and pucker his big lips around a flowering thistle. He sniffed every creek, every trickle of water, and let low tree branches brush the horseflies off his rump. One afternoon a sudden storm came in. Ground lightning swept down a meadow, up Blue's legs, through my feet, and a white ball bounced off the tops of our heads. Blue stood dazed and paralyzed. His eyes had rolled back and his big ears had laid down on either side of his head. I leaned down to look at his face. "Are you still alive?" I asked. Then he snorted, coughed, and continued on down the mountain.

One year we wintered in another town. Blue was pastured alone, which he hated, as do all horses, being extraordinarily sociable beings. The highway was being widened that year. And without my consent, they took the horse pasture fence down along the highway. When someone called and mentioned that my horse was loose along the highway, I ran out to find him. There he was, standing with his head resting against a telephone pole, so lonely, I imagined, that he was listening in on others' conversations. The fact that the fence was gone never fazed him.

Blue loved hanging out with people. If the kitchen door was left open, he'd come right in, helping himself to dog food, cookies, and apples. He was used to being fed from a sheepwagon's Dutch door. One night I came home and he was in the kitchen. My dog, Rusty, was gazing lovingly at Blue, who had just consumed a fifty-pound bag of kibbles.

Blue's sociability was ultimately his demise. One spring, he was turned out with a bunch of dude horses. One of them, Sticker, was "proud cut"—that is, he still thought he was a stallion. Apparently, he fought with Blue and Blue lost. He was found with his back leg hanging—a clean break just above the hock. There was nothing to be done.

We gave Blue a sky burial on the little knob at the southern edge of the ranch, just beyond the lake. He was facing east, toward the rising sun. For weeks I could smell his decomposing flesh. I wanted it that way. I wanted his death to sift into me just as his cranky, faithful, devilish life had seeped into my bones. After that, I bought better-looking, fancy-bred horses. But it's Blue who I miss, who I long for. No one else would have put up with him. The same has been said of me. That was our secret and the core of our annual spring pact: that if I tolerated him, he'd do the same for me.

glory days

MAXINE KUMIN

Lobbying for a pony at the age of five, stealing my brothers' camp blankets to spread on the rumps of the last few delivery-wagon horses of my suburban childhood when I was eight or nine—was there ever a time when I was not obsessed with horses? Finally, the year I turned ten, I was grudgingly allotted one hour a week on the bony back of a school horse at the local riding stable. As soon as I could demonstrate my ability to wield a manure fork and scrub saddle soap into ancient tack, I made myself so useful there that the owner/trainer gave me free lessons in return for my in-kind contribution.

It is really no surprise that I have filled up my adult life with horses. But my unrequited longing to own a horse was not gratified until I was an old married person, mother of three. We were country folk by then, having bought a derelict dairy farm and a pair of ponies for our middle child, who was not to be deprived as I was.

A friend and I went halves on the purchase of a horse from the slaughterer; we bought her by the pound for $300. A year later, after she had proved herself a runaway in the company of other horses, I bought back my friend's share. Unwilling to concede defeat (for by now, of course, I loved her), I bred this troubled mare of mixed ancestry to a local Arabian stallion. I did not know then that I was embarking on an enterprise that would absorb me year after year.

Our first filly, the daughter of that first rescued mare, is now our old-lady broodmare of twenty-two years. She is herself the mother of two fillies. I treasure the gratification of having loved and cared for three generations of a line that would otherwise have gone to the killers. They are feisty, full of opinions, possess enormous stamina, and are ours for life.

A few years after that first purchase, we heard about another mare—a registered Standardbred who had failed to prove herself at the track—being held in durance vile. Our vet accompanied us to investigate the circumstance, and he agreed that she was not likely to last the winter in that place. A little money changed hands and we came away with a barely broke four-year-old who was terrified of trailers and trembled at the touch of a man.

After using her for several years as a competitive trail horse, I bred her to a fine Arabian stallion and she foaled a handsome chestnut colt, who has served as surrogate uncle to all the subsequent babies. Two years later, she delivered a big bay filly. In the intervening years we managed to raise two more fillies, half quarter horse, half Thoroughbred, out of a dear, calm mare we had had for several years.

One May, the quarterhorse mare and the Standardbred mare delivered their foals within twenty-four hours of each other, even though their actual due dates were two weeks apart. Once the mothers had grown slightly casual about their youngsters, we were able to turn both sets of Madonnas-and-child out in the same green pasture with run-in shed. I spent hours in that upper pasture, mesmerized by the acrobatics, the joyful balletic horsing around of these two stilt-legged darlings while their complacent dams grazed side by side, lifting their heads every so often to make sure their offspring were still in sight. The Standardbred mare was such a welcoming mother that she was once observed suckling the wrong foal, an event so historic that I ran for the camera.

One breeding led to another; a lovely Arab pony mare came to live with us after her family could no longer keep her. There was no shortage of eager Arabian stallions. For my part, knowing a foal was due in late April turned the cruel pages of winter that much more easily.

Putting all my foal-watchings together, I calculate I spent at least three months of my life in a sleeping bag atop the sawdust piled in the one straight stall we use as a bin for bedding. It abuts the foaling stall, which makes it ideal for the vigil keeper. Overhead, there's a place to hang up a trouble light to read by, or to turn on at 2 A.M. when awakened by the sounds of labor beginning: the restless circling, flopping down, getting up, more circling, and finally, the bursting of the membranes that herald the actual birth.

I once logged twenty-one successive nights in the barn waiting for an overdue baby. My situation was desperate. Mosquitoes were arriving in battalions; I couldn't even read in bed. Still, I was determined to stick it out. Although most foals arrive under cover of darkness, this pony mare simply walked into the barn at midmorning with one infant hoof already in this world, plopped herself down, and in less than one minute delivered her filly.

Now that we've stopped breeding, I acknowledge the comfort of my own bed throughout April and May. No more restless nights overhearing the rustle of hay, the snores of dozing equines, the arisings and the folding in again of legs, as I wait in a state of exalted terror for the moment of birth. But winter is longer than ever now. I miss those glory days of spring foals.

sparky moves to manhattan

Sparky was a generous gift from friends: a Peruvian Paso colt with top bloodlines, strong conformation, uncanny intelligence, and a serious penchant for unruly behavior. In all my years with horses I had never encountered such a rebellious creature. While my family was plotting his demise, I was planning to make him a respectable member of society. Sparky just needed to find a purpose in life.

Well, ten years and many "purposes" later, Sparky has finally discovered his true destiny: acting. He's not just a trick horse; he's a thespian, and he truly loves to perform. His first starring role is in "Sparky Moves to Manhattan," a comedy about moving from the suburbs of Los Angeles to New York City. The following video prints tell a bit of the story and give a glimpse of Sparky's newfound talent.

1

DEBBIE SHOWS SPARKY PHOTOS OF NY

SPARKY IS MOVING TO MANHATTAN

SPARKY IS NOT HAPPY ABOUT THE MOVE

HE BEGS THOMAS TO GO WITH HIM

SPARKY HAS A NIGHTMARE . . .

HE'S MUGGED BY NEW YORK THUGS

SPARKY DOESN'T WANT TO LEAVE

DEBBIE & SPARKY SHARE A TENDER MOMENT

REALITY STRIKES: SPARKY IS NOT

TCR 14:06.27.24
PLAY   LOCK

FLYING FIRST CLASS - HE'S GOING CARGO

SPARKY DEMONSTRATES A GOOD SAFETY RULE:

TCR 10:05.30.10
REC   LOCK

DON'T GO INTO A VEHICLE WITH STRANGERS

"LURING ME WITH TREATS?"

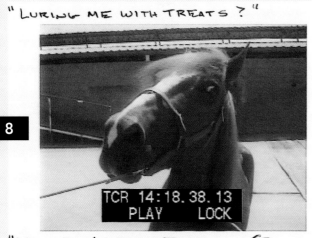

TCR 14:18.38.13
PLAY   LOCK

"WHAT DO YOU THINK I AM ... STUPID?"

SPARKY & PRINCESS IN THE TRAILER

TCR 13:05.40.25
PLAY   LOCK

SPARKY MAKES A NEW FRIEND

AMSTERDAM AVENUE

10

`16:05:38:11`

SPARKY ARRIVES IN MANHATTAN

SPARKY UNLOADS AT A BUS STOP

11

`16:07:01:05`

ON THE UPPER WEST SIDE

SPARKY ENTERS HIS NEW "HIGH-RISE"

12

`19:13:56:24`

"THIS IS REALLY WEIRD!"

SPARKY IN HIS 2ND FLOOR STALL

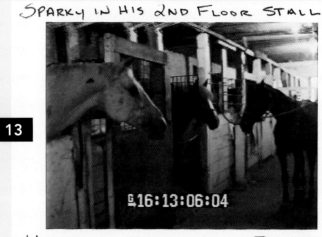

13

`16:13:06:04`

HE MAKES FRIENDS WITH BUSTER

SPARKY & BUSTER ON STREETS OF NY

THEY WAIT TO CROSS CENTRAL PARK WEST

CENTRAL PARK - TAKING A BREAK

SPARKY DOWNS A SODA

SPARKY STROLLS THROUGH CENTRAL

PARK - SO MANY SIGHTS TO SEE!

SPARKY DISCOVERS THAT NY IS

MORE THAN JUST CONCRETE & SKYSCRAPERS

big

JONIS AGEE

It was a good time in my life. Springtime. I was getting married, getting a new husband, a new life. My daughter was in college and we had finally worked out most of our issues. We were friends now. My writing was beginning to get noticed. I felt younger than I had in years, and best of all, my soon-to-be-husband promised to buy me a new horse. I'd sold the last one the previous fall and had been having horse dreams every night for months. Then a friend told me that Richard, or Ricky as the owner called him, was for sale. There he was, a sixteen-three appendix quarter horse so dark brown he was almost black. In fact, his show name was Black Tie, and by the last show in October his coat would glisten black. I remembered seeing him at the previous fall show waiting at the entrance to the hippodrome on the Minnesota State Fair Grounds for the amateur hunter formal attire class, calmly elegant, self-assured as an older brother to the smaller, lighter thoroughbreds around him. I envied the owner that day. There's almost no envy like horse envy. It takes you right back to those early childhood days of dreaming your way into horses through books and pictures and play.

But he'd fallen from grace. Stuck in the two-horse trailer, he shoved his big brown nose out of the opening in front and got a whack for it. "Dickhead," Nori said. I wanted to apologize to him for his owner's bad behavior, but without hesitation he put it out again and she laughed and rubbed it, which seemed to satisfy him. He wasn't the kind to hold a grudge. When Nori unloaded him, he had dust on his rump and a piece of hay in his tail. He didn't shine enough and his equipment was dull with sweat and dirt. The clipping he'd recently had left several long spines on his chin like a catfish and tufts of hair notching his ears like a badly trimmed yard. He was braided, though, and his thick long neck arched as he nuzzled my outstretched hand.

"He likes anybody," Nori explained, and I felt that weird ambivalence that comes from childhood when you imagine owning the horse nobody else can ride, the one who loves you and only you. "Anybody can ride him, too. My groom won in Chicago on him." She kicked the ground with the toe of her boot and dirt chunked on his leg. He wrinkled his shoulder to dislodge a fly and pulled enough rope out of her hand to crop at some grass.

"He's big," I said and patted him, unable to see over the back. Just the way I like my horses.

"Yeah, well, he may be sold." Nori slapped at a fly on his haunch with the end of the lead rope and I felt my day dim a little.

The saga of the sale went on for over a month. Nori's father was furious that this twenty-thousand-dollar horse was such a flop. Her trainer had tried everything he could think of and some more, then moved

Ricky to the back of the barn where his failure would be out of sight. Nori stopped riding him. In between trying to finish the year of teaching at my college and carry out the final planning for the marriage the day after classes were done in mid-May, I would get phone calls from my friend who was acting as the Henry Kissinger of horse negotiations. I kept assuring her that I couldn't afford the horse, and she kept reporting new concessions in pricing. I wondered when the assumption that this was the horse for me took over. I'd never even ridden him.

But his image was in my mind now. He was the horse that galloped across my dreams at night as I indeed did get married, my hands shaking so hard the rose and lily bouquet started losing petals halfway down the aisle, leaving me standing in a puddle of white and yellow at the altar, and my jaw clenched so tight the words to the hymns came out half a phrase too late as we sat side by side in the little choir pew while the congregation of friends and family stared at us during the hour-long Episcopalian service. Sitting up there, I had to wonder how I came to be married in a religion neither of us had ever been part of. But then it was over, and after the fight about who was to blame for the lack of honeymoon plans, we were driving north with no reservations to the Lake Superior shoreline and the boundary waters between Minnesota and Canada. It was a strange trip, one of those times when you discover too much and too little about the person you're with. Although I'm terrified of water, my husband, Paul, insisted we take a canoe across the lake at Gunflint Lodge with waters so dark you couldn't see more than an inch down its icy one-hundred-fifty-foot depth, and so choppy I was half sobbing crouched paddling in the bow of the boat as the waves broke over me. My husband sat in the back without a life jacket because he wasn't chicken. I remembered the old movie of *Moby Dick* with Gregory Peck and thought for sure I'd die, partly because that idiot behind me would drown without a life preserver. But that was nothing compared to Thunder Bay. Okay, I admit that I often go places because I love the sound of the name and I'd insisted. The hotel at Thunder Bay had as little to offer as the town, small, dingy, the air conditioner pumping out warm air soaked with years of stale beer and cigarette smoke. We took turns getting out of the lumpy bed and going for walks to the lobby to sit and wait for sleep again all night long. Then I called home and there was a message to call my friend immediately. Did I want the horse? The price was rock bottom, but still just past what I knew we could afford. I didn't look at the dark circles under my husband's eyes or the boyish swoop of black hair on his forehead that had made me love him to begin with, I just said yes. I had to. And in that one act I changed our lives forever.

⌒⌒⌒

The first thing I did was ride Richard. He felt solid and competent. Testing me, he refused to take a canter cue for a while, then popped into it when he decided I'd had enough. The fences came up easily. No big deal, his attitude said, relax, trust me. So I hung on to his mane and let him do the work. I'd been jumping for a couple of years but had been pushed too quickly and overfaced by a poor trainer, so now I was scared to death but determined to keep trying. I'd never felt so safe before. The trainer made me try another horse, a better jumper, but it was a small, quick mare who wore her nerves on the skin the same as me. By the end we were both sweated up, and I knew Ricky was my horse.

We had to take a bank loan. I admit it, I held my husband's feet to the fire. He'd promised. After the canoe trip across that lake, I thought he owed me something. Moreover, there was no way I wasn't going to have this horse. Everything else was working out so well, I believed there was some kind of fate at work—some kind of good fate for a change.

Then a few weeks later my older sister died tragically. I was so shaken I would begin crying driving down the street in the middle of traffic. It was as if all the stops, all the infrastructure of my life were wiped out in a common disaster of weather. I'd grown up in tornado alley, Omaha, so I expected the sky to darken and swoop down on us, but nothing was as shocking as her loss. If I hadn't been able to drive to the barn each morning and spend those hours with Richard, with his large brown hide as the wordless comfort I needed, I'd still be sitting at some traffic light in Minneapolis waiting for the emptiness to replace her memory. While the other riders and stable help were away at shows and jobs, Richard and I would be the only ones in the cool dark barn, the flies slowly bumping and buzzing against the windows, the birds in the oak trees out front whistling and calling while I cleaned and rubbed and polished that coat so it was flawless and bright.

That first month I took lessons and worked long hours on flat riding with my stirrups tied or taken off, trying to perfect my position and help the horse develop his own balance. He had this trick when we got in tight or I was uncertain at a fence: He would take a quick trot step. It frustrated both of us. If I could sit still and keep my leg tight, he would maintain his pace, but the minute I shifted or my errant hands took over, we got that step. By July I was ready for my first show, though. The old owner, Nori, was there; my old trainer, friends, and half the world, it seemed, stood around the ring. We made our circle and cantered to the first fence. I remember those three rounds as the most comfortable I ever felt as Richard cantered around the ring. We won two classes and were reserve champion in our division. I keep a snapshot of us going over a fence in my office at the university now, the only one. Richard's ears are up, his knees not so tight as he lopes the low rails, and maybe I look tense and too posed; you can always pick a good thing apart, I've discovered, the way the trainer would wait outside the ring and tell me the little mistakes I'd made. Still, it was in many ways the best day of our life together, how we surprised each other.

That's when we discovered Richard's sense of humor, too. Although Paul was a novice, he wanted to ride. I put him on top with a lead rope in the closed indoor arena early the next morning. While I watched, Richard plodded faithfully around the ring, but the minute I left them alone, he went to the corner and stood facing the metal walls, pretending he didn't understand any of the signals my frantic husband was giving. Later, Richard

would try other pranks including lifting his tail for a load on my head when I was trimming his back ankles if I wasn't careful. He'd try to pull the handkerchief out of the farrier's back pocket while being shod and slip his halter in long hauls in my trailer. And he had a bit of the bully in him. I could never tell whether he was playing or serious when a smaller or younger horse would be coming toward us in the ring and he would bulge over and flatten his ears and snap his teeth like a dog in the other horse's direction. Over the long Minnesota winters, he managed to intimidate at least one or two horses to a complete stop every time they saw him coming.

In summer pastures, he played the father or the king, whichever struck his mood, to the younger, less dominant animals. He wasn't one of those horses who are so aggressive, they're dangerous, though. Richard was a big presence and he simply wanted to take up the space he needed. Sometimes he just needed more. He was self-reliant, too. Not the sort to whinny and fret when stable-mates left or he was alone. He always assumed he was unforgettable, and he was. Not because he was the flashiest, most talented horse on the circuit, but because of something else. He was the Tommy Lee Jones of horses, not so handsome, not so much the leading man, but the character with strength and versatility. He didn't suck back, he never quit at a fence, he made things work out no matter what the rider did. He did his job, he always did his job. He was what they called a packer, worth his weight in golden oats.

And he was always happy to see me, coming when I called him, no matter how green and sweet the grass was. There are some horses as temperamental as divas, but Richard was the other sort. When the barn help played rock and roll while they fed and cleaned stalls, he bopped his head up and down in time with the music while they laughed and sang along. He liked being fussed over by the hour while he grazed or dozed. He even tolerated my training on him in the winter, hauling him to dressage instructors who tried to get him off his forehand, to use his hind end more. He'd try anything. I don't remember him ever being afraid, no matter what I did. He trusted us humans, he believed in us. No matter who got on him, Richard would march down to the fences and jump. When he got hurt, he knew we would help him. Once he'd been rubbing his tail against the tailboard in the trailer and gotten two big splinters I didn't know about. A couple of weeks later I noticed he was scratching his hind end against things a lot, and so I gave him a bath and started to work on combing out his thick long tail. Richard kept twisting his tail toward me and shifting his haunches against me whenever I thought I was finished. It took me a while of working up the tailbone, following his signals to find the infected splinters and squeeze them out. After I cleaned and medicated the wounds, he looked at me and blew hard through his nose as if to say, *Well, it took you a while.*

He made friends with my husband, too. They compromised on the riding business—Paul could lead Richard to big clumps of grass or hand-feed him hay and brush him while the eating went on. When they were done, Richard would rest his big head on Paul's shoulder and close his eyes like a giant dog. I don't think my husband has ever been that close to another creature. Usually a quiet man in public, the one topic that could get him going was Richard. He even brought pictures to show his family the first time we went home.

Then my first two collections of short stories came out two years later, and I began traveling to give readings. Since that first summer Paul had lost his grandfather, then a brother, too, after I lost my sister. We were both stunned with grief in our lives, unable to speak to each other some days, for fear of what we couldn't stop ourselves from saying.

The call came on a Monday morning. Richard had spiked a temperature and was severely dehydrated. I should meet him at the vet clinic. He was cross-tied in the metal stocks, hooked up to an IV with three assistants pouring water into him via a tube down his throat. He looked at me with wild eyes, pleading it seemed as he lifted one leg after another and stretched to pee brown fluid every few minutes as if he were tying up. "Toxic shock," the vet said. I kept shaking my head and trying to soothe Richard, who didn't seem able to hear my voice. There was nothing they could do; he was only getting worse. The leg, the mysterious infection, he was dying. The trainer showed up and told me what we needed to do. I waited for a miracle, called Paul but had to leave a message. Then I said good-bye to Richard. The trainer said it was better not to be there when they injected him, and I listened to her, which I will always regret. "You'll have that image of him down in your mind if you stay," she said. "It's better to remember him as alive and happy." Instead, I have the image now of his agony, unrelieved by the people he'd trusted, frantic, trying to break loose of us once and for all. I tried to apologize to him as I said good-bye, but I don't think he heard me.

When I called Nori, she broke down and cried. And in the fall when she saw the woman who'd bred and raised him, that person broke down and cried, too. The groom who had cared for him and braided his mane at shows quit the show circuit and went back to finish school and go on to vet school so she could figure out what caused the toxic shock that destroyed his kidneys and liver. He was the kind of horse who had that affect on you. A joker, a friend, a character. Not the greatest athlete, not the flashiest, showiest animal but a big-hearted horse with a soul who accepted and loved all of us, whether we deserved it or not.

After Richard died, everything changed, of course. When we separated, Paul said that of all the deaths we'd shared those few years of marriage, Richard's was the hardest loss, the one that broke his heart. I don't think either one of us ever felt the same after that. Since then

I've published two novels and even had two other horses. But it has never been the same. Sometimes you can't replace what has gone from your life, I discovered. Sometimes you lose something forever. I've never trusted another horse to carry me safely around a jumping course, never found another friend quite like Richard. Maybe I never want to, either. I can't say. The horse dreams come back now and then, sticking around for a month or two, then disappearing again when they go unanswered. A couple of weeks ago, I got out my show bridle, the one with the brass nameplate at the crown, and hung it on the wall next to my easy chair. Maybe that's to say it's an artifact now, too, or maybe it's to try to awaken in me what I lost and continue to lose not being in the company of horses anymore. Or maybe it's that I can finally start to love Richard again, not just grieve for him, but love him in a way he would probably appreciate—by finding another big brown four-legged friend to bully and cajole me down the road. I don't know anymore, I just don't.

ROBIN SCHWARTZ

the arabber series

A photographer friend introduced me to the Retreat Street Stables in Baltimore: horses, ponies, goats, and dogs in the middle of an urban city—this animal photographer's dream situation. I had been photographing stray and "junkyard" dogs for ten years (dogs continue to be principal subjects for me), and I'd recently embarked on a project with primates.

But my connection with the stables went further, into my own family history. I grew up on the same plot of land as my grandfather. He had been a junk man with a horse and wagon. Our wagon wheel remained in our yard and a lot of the horse stuff still cluttered our lofted barn, then called the garage. My grandfather, who lived next door, used to baby-

Father holding son on Sundance

sit me. He had been run over by a wagon when my father was seven years old. This head injury ended his career as a carpenter, and after that everyone treated him like a child. He was nicer than all the adults I knew, especially my tough grandmother. Grandpa Jake was kind to animals, and animals have been my passion ever since I can remember. He died when I was almost seven, and my dad died when I was nineteen. Seeing the men in Baltimore's Retreat Street Stables—a rundown place, like our garage—with their cart horses was wonderful, and I felt an immediate connection to their world. There were so many similarities between the two places; I found marbles in each.

Originally Baltimore had sixty-five stables. I located the last existing five stables through the local folklore society. I visited all the stables, photographing at each location, though a lot of my shooting occurred at Retreat Street, where most of the kids seemed to congregate, and at the Calhoun Street Stables, where the fruit-and-vegetable trucks are stationed for produce pickup. There I met Poppa Cabbage and his beautiful blue-eyed pony, Bo, a very nice, hard-working man who spared the time for my photographs; and Mr. Blair, the man who taught horseback riding, even to me.

The men at the stable bartered with the local kids: clean up the stables in exchange for rides. Most of the boys were ten to thirteen, except for a few older teenage boys, who knew more and had more responsibilities. One of the teenagers, Eddy, was saving up $400 for his own horse. I became an honorary boy (I was a match in height) and took my riding lessons on China Doll, a safe, patient white pony with big eyes. It was a fantastic, exhilarating feeling to ride on the city streets in Baltimore alongside buses.

Castle Point Stable

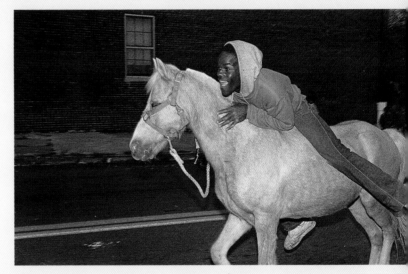

Harry riding

Marlon riding

Lavle and Arabber cart horse

Preparing to race

Anthony and Shadow

Marlon

rescue

LUCY GREALY

The last thing I remember is Lisa riding Eddie past me at a canter, something I'd specifically asked her not to do and for exactly this reason: The next thing I remember is Cocoa's hoof precisely in front of my face. I was on the ground, I knew that much, the wet, coarse sand in my mouth, pinching my ear. The sand was wet enough that when Cocoa's hoof pressed into it I could see bubbles of water pressing out around her heel, which was thick and creased and about four inches from my nose. Her hoof must have landed there, but I do not remember that part, and it must have lifted off almost immediately, but these comings and goings didn't matter. Her hoof was simply there. I did not yet understand that my body was laid up on the fence, my awkward feet in the air, that it was only

my head on the ground. I turned my eyes and looked up, following the line of her leg from this heel up to her muddy elbows, which I hadn't cleaned properly before saddling her, her belly all wet from the puddles we'd splashed through. Cocoa had a bit of a hay belly, and I saw now how clearly round and long it was, how perfect. My eyes kept following her body up, discovering the subtle, secret line of flesh that shows itself where one half of the body meets the other, how this line extended itself from her white, hairless belly button to the dark, soft mounds of her udder. Her back legs were part of the line now, too, though I could see only one leg all the way to the tip of its hoof, stretching and pointing up, like an arm when an unusual plane passed by, to the white, just-rained sky. "Hmmmm," was all I could think to myself.

We all knew Cocoa bucked, and bucked like a pro, when given even the slightest chance. I rode her anyway. Like all the horses at the stable, she had come from the auction, that Wednesday night squalor filled with dog food dealers, alcoholic cowboys, and almost-broke hack barn owners. Each week we begged Mr. Evans to let us go with him, "we" being the various broken-homed children, future alcoholics ourselves, who worked at Mr. Evans' rat-infested hack barn in exchange for free riding. Cocoa was named Cocoa because of her chocolate-colored spots. I rode her even though she bucked because I imagined I could tame her, that she bucked because she was unhappy. I would make her happy: I would let her know by bringing her carrots, by brushing her, by putting my small, thin arms around her neck, by avoiding all of her "triggers," by telling her that I understood what it was to be unhappy. "I'd buck, too," I confided in her.

She never stopped bucking. Mr. Evans, fearing a lawsuit, put her back in the trailer a few Wednesdays later. I wasn't there when they took her away. I went back to Boone, a mild-mannered Appaloosa I loved more than life itself, but who I understood would never amount to all that much. All the time that Cocoa was at the stable, all the while that I was dreaming she was the special, great horse that would somehow, inexplicably, like The Pie in *National Velvet,* turn all of this failure around, I paid Boone some extra love so he wouldn't be jealous.

Each of us there, unable to afford our own horses and too ignorant to get "proper" jobs at "proper" stables, fell in love with different horses from the auction by turn. Ray, who'd been there the longest, got to pick which horse was

"his" when a new selection arrived, then Lori did, then Lisa, who already "had" Eddie, and so on down the hierarchical line. I was very near the bottom. The horses I picked, like Boone, or which any of us picked really, in the end broke our hearts simply because we had to watch them be worked half to death, their mouths pulled and their sides kicked by huge city louts out for a cheap day in the country. Or, like Cocoa, they broke my heart because they had something "wrong" with them that, no matter how hard I tried to fix it, spelled out their eventual leaving.

The people who came out from they city rarely got their money's worth. Though some horses, like Boone, were well-behaved, their goodness only made it harder for them: Hackers ran them into the ground. They would bring the horses back heaving, covered with sweat, foam dripping down from under the saddle, and tell us what a great time they had. If this was done to "your" horse, everyone else understood and wouldn't make fun of you, which was par for the course the rest of the time, if you hid in the tack room and cried. Most horses, however, wised up pretty quick.

The stables were at the bottom of a gently sloping hill, and the trail wound its way up this hill. For the first half mile the hackers and their horses were in plain view, and the horses, however grudgingly, plodded forward. But then the trail turned and became obscured by trees, and the horses understood the exact spot at which they could stop in their tracks and start eating leaves. Most people who came to our stable didn't have a clue about riding, and all their yanking and kicking meant nothing to the horses. Soon they'd start calling for help. Secretly proud of the horses, we'd ignore the hackers' cries for help unless Mr. Evans was around, in which case we'd take turns going up and "rescuing" the riders. At least a few times on a busy day people demanded their money back.

"These horses don't go!" they'd shout at Mr. Evans.

"You just can't ride, that's the problem."

"I can too ride, I took lessons at camp. These horses suck. They won't move."

At this point, Mr. Evans would turn and hope I was around, because I was the most effective member of the crew for this particular stunt.

"I bet that skinny little girl could get this horse to go."

It was true: I was painfully skinny and underdeveloped, despite the fact that I was fourteen. My body was an embarrassment most of the time, but as I stepped up to the horse while its rider clumsily climbed down, I understood my scrawny shape worked in my favor sometimes. There was a terrible intimacy just then between me and whatever horse was starting a nervous jig at the end of the reins held tight by Mr. Evans. The horse knew the routine, and even though it was the horse's well-being on the line just then, I hoped, I felt practically sure, that the horse understood my actual, my real role in all of this. Though anyplace was better than being at home, the stable was not an easy place to spend time; my fingers swelled and turned so useless in the winter that I couldn't undress myself afterwards in the garage, where my mother made me go because I was so dirty, while in the summer the hay stuck like needles to my drenched shirt, sticking me whenever I lifted my arms over my head or tried to lean back in a moment of rest. I was working the work of a grown man for no pay, was bullied by the older kids for my assorted physical and emotional shames, and my romantic heart cringed at the sight of each broken-down horse, but still I did not know how to find, or even name, any other place to be.

As I walked toward that horse it eyed me with a knowing and a tension that reminded me of the auctions on Wednesdays. For me, the excitement of that place was intense. All those human voices rising and converging in the air over our heads, punctuated by the loud shrill whinnies that horses make when they're in a strange place. You always had to be careful standing next to a horse's head then, because he could let out one of those piercing calls right in your eardrum if you weren't observant enough to see it coming. Most of the horses there were destined for "the meat man," but it was something other than their physical worth to humans that thrilled me when they whinnied. Each horse had its own way of letting you know it was about to call out, but usually their ears pitched straight forward, the tail held high, their neck just starting to arch, the horizontal line of muscles just starting to show on their belly as they took a deep breath. When I saw those moves, I took half a step back and watched the horse whinny, its eyes large, its mouth half open, its nostrils so wide you could see all the color inside. Something wild about them, something that had nothing to do with any of us humans, with the various shapes of our own sadnesses that we forced upon them, shone at that moment.

While the customer watched, while everyone watched, the first problem now was to prevent the horse from running off up the trail at full gallop before I could even get on. The horse turned in nervous circles every time I put one foot up, causing me to hop around in a comic dance. But once up in the saddle, and without bothering to put my feet in the stirrups, all I had to do was point the animal beneath me in the right direction and off we'd go with a clattering of hooves, leaving everyone behind to stand on the dry and rocky ground, the quick four-beat gait smooth as anything, the wind pulling at my shirt. I liked to glance down and see the hard, packed dirt of the trail slip beneath us, the galloping horse's leg reaching out as if to grab that ground and pull it toward us, while if I dipped my head just right the leaves of a few low branches caressed the top of my hair. This was the moment I dreamed of, always, before I had ever been on a horse, and it was this moment I would keep dreaming of all my adult life. Galloping up and away in a smooth commotion of silent, stopped-time thrill: It was this moment exactly, except that I wanted it someplace else, under different circumstances; this moment exactly, but

in a different moment. If I had my own horse, if I could become rich and rescue Boone from this grassless place, or if I could become smart enough and good enough to rescue a horse like Cocoa, if I could transform her into something "right," or if for some sudden and miraculous reason whatever horse I was on could suddenly really *want* to be stretching forward like this, out into what seemed like an endless chance, then I could live in this quick, enraptured moment forever. For now, for effect, I held the reins as lightly as possible, and maybe I'd spin the horse around a couple of times at the end of the visible trail, then gallop back down to the stable, pull up short and hop off with a nonchalant air that told every-one I didn't care a stick.

"See," Mr. Evans would say, turning to the silenced customer.

PATRICIA CRONIN

pony tales

I grew up In New England: Massachusetts, Maine, and Rhode Island. I never rode as a child, although I had my own imaginary horse that I rode around my grandparents' backyard. I obsessively drew horses and wrote poems about them colliding in the sky with brilliant colors around them.

Returning to this subject matter as an adult, and subsequently learning how to ride, is like reliving the adolescence I never had and fulfilling a dream deferred.

Top Shelf, 1996

Piper, 1996

Harmony, 1996

Piper, 1996

Dandy, 1996

Vamp, 1996

Parfait Prince, 1996

Aurora, 1996

impossible horses

TOM RABBITT

When I was a kid I used to run away from home. The first time I was almost five, the summer before I began kindergarten. A few years later a couple of my attempts were serious. Once I tried to walk from Boston to Cape Cod. I got about twenty-five miles before I was found by the police. If only I'd known about hitchhiking. I had no answer for my parents when they asked me what I thought I was doing. I know I wasn't a happy camper, and I suppose that even then I wanted to make some sort of escape, to see other parts of the world, to find a new life. Recently I tried again—and again I ran away to the

beach. After twenty-five years in Alabama, I told myself, I was at last going to see the fabulous Redneck Riviera.

As I drove I rehearsed my childish lamentations. My life had become a series of melodramatic catastrophes—a broken foot, a scratched cornea, a dead-end job, a desk littered with rejection slips. With existential self-regard, I believed I faced a crisis. A post-midlife crisis. Something to contemplate at the beach.

At school, when I limped by in my cast, when I squinted out of my swollen eye, I was sure my colleagues smiled too broadly. They had always known that my destiny was suspect, that my career was as broken as my foot, that in the noisy hallways I was a foolish figure, ridiculous, maybe even a bit pathetic, a single man with too many pets and a few unsavory friends and no family within a thousand miles, a man obviously too old to ride horses or to jog on Tuscaloosa's shady streets. I saw in those censorious professorial faces the same look I had seen through the cracked windshield of the hit-and-run car as it took the intersection from me that bright spring morning. Took the right-of-way and left me with a broken foot.

For four weeks my foot was in a cast. I could neither run nor ride, and I was growing fat and frustrated. I needed to be working with a young mare I had in training for the Bonanza classes at the Arabian Region Twelve Show. She's a good mare. In the hands of our trainer she won the state Three-Year-Old Halter Futurity and then, the next year, the two of them won the Western Pleasure Maturity. The mare and I had qualified for regionals by winning our first class with me in the saddle: Amateur Hunt Seat, Riders over Forty. I am well over forty. For the Bonanza we were entered in Hunt Seat, Western Pleasure and Trail. Trail was going to be the problem; just that first task—getting through the gate—was still more than we could handle. My broken foot had cost us a month's work. Something for a man to resent when he is well over forty.

The cast was removed on a Thursday morning. I rode that afternoon. The trainer had us practice backing through a pattern and sidepassing along the rail. We made a little progress. I rode again on Friday and Satur-

day. In our session on Monday the mare went over backwards with me. The wreck was caused by another horse that, under a weak rider, while passing us in the arena, wheeled and attacked, ears pinned, teeth bared, as if it were another of the wild delegates of fate. My mare backpedaled until she lost her balance. Too much practice? At least I had had the sense to head her into the rail; had I not, she would have crushed both of us against it. I climbed back on, because that is what a rider is supposed to do, what I've always done, and I rode her for a little while longer. Both of us were sore. Fortunately, I had been wearing my safety helmet. All in all, we were lucky nothing else but our confidence had been broken. Her body, from head to hip, had pinned me head to foot to the ground. From aching head to mended foot. When I rode her a couple of days later, our companion in the ring was a pony. My mare flinched whenever it approached. I could feel her tension even if our trainer couldn't see it, and I'm sure the mare felt my own apprehension as we fed one another's fear. Still, we kept working. For a week I deluded myself into believing that there was yet enough time. The delusion of every life.

I bought my first horse almost exactly twenty-five years ago. I was finishing graduate school in Iowa and was on my way to Alabama. A friend took me to the monthly auction at Kalona, in Amish country. Shrewdly, if not wisely, the concession stand sold beer. I bid twenty-six dollars for an orphan foal and he was mine. I brought him south in a stall I built in the back of a U-Haul truck.

Dog, cat, horse, furniture —that's what the Indiana highway patrolman saw when he stopped me for a defective taillight. At that point, he hadn't seen everything. Nor had I. That colt never amounted to much. But I bought other horses. Then, with my first book advance, I made a down payment on a small farm. After a few years I bought a larger place. I had dreams of raising fine horses, supporting myself and my dreams.

For years the horses and the land kept me broke and tired and a bit crazy. The dreams of course gave way to work and worry, the necessities of life. I don't mean to sound histrionic or excessively romantic, but the horses—their beauty, my love for them and my unavoidable responsibilities to them—kept me alive by keeping me anchored in place. I was pledged to them and to the land. Like matrimony. Or holy orders. A kind of sacramental vow, I think.

⌒∿⌒

A year ago the financial pressure got to be too much. I faced bankruptcy, so I sold the last farm and most of the livestock. I moved myself to a nice old house in town. The remaining horses—I have six now—board at a stable less than ten minutes away. Incredibly, the new life has turned out to be less expensive in almost every way. Now I don't have to get up before daybreak to feed and clean stalls. In the evenings I don't have to drive twenty miles back to the country to feed and then return to town to hear yet another poetry reading. I don't have to haul feed or hay or shavings. I don't have to bush-hog pastures or spread fertilizer or fix fences. I don't have to worry about drunk hunters shooting my horses or Mr. Tilley killing another of my dogs. Now I get to ride— broken bones permitting—as often as I want. I get to travel, to satisfy that old urge. I took my first overseas trip at Christmas—to horse-mad Ireland, home of my grandparents, source of my own genetic craziness.

Then, for the first time, I went to the beach at Gulf Shores. Of course, I wanted to get away, to nurse my wounds, to discover that I do have a plan of some sort. After all, I thought, soon enough I'll be ready to retire. Perhaps I'd like to move to the coast. Get a weathered house on a windswept dune. Maybe keep one horse. Ride on the beaches. Or maybe sell every last one of them. Spend my life like an old surfer following waves from beach to beach.

I got out of town just ahead of one those frontal systems that, like spiteful deities, spread their satisfactions across the Savage South. Thunderstorms and tornadoes lashed Huntsville and Decatur. Soon enough they would reach Birmingham and Tuscaloosa. Sunshowers dropped through lowering clouds, green light reflected off the wet asphalt, the devil beat his wife over the semis racing on the two-lane highway. After I crossed Mobile Bay I took the scenic route, the coast road through heavenly, expensive Fairhope and past the truly Grand Hotel at Point Clear. I saw many nice houses for sale, all of them more than I could ever afford. Beyond these well-manicured floral tributes to good taste lay mile after endless mile of cottages up on stilts. Clever mailboxes and driftwood deer. The last of the wooded shoreline was divided into lots and put up for sale. Men with chain saws were taking down the last scrub pines. I saw nine miles of strip mall hell from Foley to Gulf Shores and then, along the barrier island, which is the Redneck Riviera, a six-lane highway ran beside the invisible beach. I supposed that the fabled white sugar sands lay somewhere behind the pale of motels and condos.

My motel room was expensive and about the size of a box stall. My view was of the parking lot, the highway, an assortment of fast-food joints and convenience stores. Behind the motel, behind the continuous barricade of condos and other motels, a narrow strip of white beach curved away. A few people strolled. A couple of dogs chased the foam. Pelicans and gulls swooped and screamed. The water looked like syrup. The air smelled brackish. Back in the motel, after dinner, I waited for the future to reveal itself. Until four the next morning the dozen or so students who had rented the rooms on either side of me partied on the balcony in front of my window. They moved away politely when I asked them—after all, I looked old and tired—but after a while they drifted back to laugh and drink and throw beer cans down on their friends in the parking lot.

I left at eight the next morning, in the middle of the slow, deliberate storm, which had finally caught up with me. Wind bent the palm trees and drove sheets of rain and sand across the six-lane. Lightning flashed in the thousands of windows looking out over the beach and the highway. I drove straight back to Tuscaloosa. Before I went to the house I stopped to see my horses.

"What are you doing here?" the barn manager asked. " I thought you went to the beach."

"I did. I didn't like it."

"Too bad," he said.

On a pretty spring Saturday afternoon a few weeks ago I drove south again, this time to yet another horse sale. I had heard that a very well-bred nine-year-old Arabian stallion was going to be dumped by his owners. The story unfolded like a Hollywood script. The horse wore no halter. He'd been run onto a cattle trailer, run off, run through the sale barn alleys into a holding chute where he whinnied and pawed, wheeled and reared.

"Don't get in there," one of the hands hollered. "He's crazy."

I went in anyway. Most people in Alabama believe all Arabians are crazy. After a few minutes the horse relaxed enough to let me lay my hands on him. I saw the scars from the barbed-wire fences he had been caught in.

"He's like to kill you," another man yelled. He sounded almost hopeful.

Perhaps if the stallion had been a crazed killer, I would have turned back and he would have been sold for dog food—despite his beauty and his pedigree. As it turned out, I bid fifteen dollars more than the meatpacker. I put a halter on the horse, led him onto a trailer and took him home. He's proven to be sensible as well as handsome. He's good enough to breed some mares to and he's easygoing enough to train for riding. He has a future— tied to mine, I guess, at least for the time being.

ROBB KENDRICK

texas, usa

puiSsance

JANE SMILEY

You can see it in the pictures. The entire being of the horse is flying forward. His ears are pricked, his gaze is focused. His knees are lifted and his elbows bent. The powerful thrust of his haunches that straightens his back legs is immediately followed by careful tucking as he brings his hooves over the obstacle. A bold and talented jumper seeks the jump, presses against the rider's hands as he accelerates toward his leap. The coiling of the approach as the spring winds itself up followed by the jolt of free energy as the horse clears the obstacle is irresistible. The rider has only to go along, but to really go along, to remain still and firm on the approach, then to accept the forward movement of the spring, heels down, head up, hands and arms yielding. Young riders, like youthful thrill seekers of all kinds, want to jump all the

time. Like any fourteen-year-old, I wanted to feel that feeling every day but also, like any forty-eight-year-old, to never jump again.

The world's record is eight feet one inch, set in 1949, the year I was born. When I imagine that jump, I imagine the horse crouched on the top of the wall like a cat, poised to spring lightly down. I simply cannot imagine a horse, a heavy-bodied animal with an immobile spine, long neck, delicate legs, and very short tail, flying out of sight over a fence taller than a doorway.

The competition is something like a human high jump competition—as the wall grows, horses are eliminated one by one until the last one over clean is declared the winner. Unlike human competition, however, the obstacle is solid. Neither horse nor rider can see over it until the rising curve of their effort shows them the landing. The rider must drive the horse rhythmically forward and then, when the arc of the horse's jump commences (described in the arc of the horse's body as the "bascule"), he or she must remain perfectly in time with the horse's dynamic center of balance, neither behind, making the horse drag his weight over the jump, nor ahead, burdening the horse's forehand as he rises over the apex of the jump.

When I was a child, I used to jump bareback over fences four to four and a half feet high. I don't remember being afraid. I think my mother took custody of the fear for me, and my job was only not to fall off and not to let on how often I was jumping. When I came back to riding at forty-four, though, every little two-foot fence looked to me like a Puissance wall. The way I prepared myself to jump a course was to not look at the ring or the jumps until I absolutely had to. Fear was a large, hollow thing inside me, steadily expanding. I was perfectly familiar with fear, but it soon became clear that for the first time in my adult life, fear might have undesirable consequences.

There are other writers like me, I know. Once I read that Jacques Derrida never leaves his office without vividly imagining the bloody car crash that will kill or maim him before he arrives home. As for P. D. James, one interviewer has reported that when James let him into her pleasant bourgeois home in its pleasant bourgeois neighborhood, she took a moment to check, quickly and suspiciously, whether any gunmen were standing around outside the door, ready to shoot. Random or intended, that part didn't matter. The question was whether, this time, one was out there. Contrary to the writer's cliché,

about the only thing that doesn't frighten me is a blank sheet of paper (though I did see a man on TV once whose paper cut had ultimately resulted in a bacterial infection that cost him all four limbs and his nose).

For years I've been as cautious about staying home as I have been about leaving, as fearful of what I might find OUT THERE as I am of what might COME AND GET ME. Fear has proved the spur to a productive imagination, and its companionship has proved tolerable, if not pleasant. I have, with perhaps ninety percent success, sent my children off on their daily walk to school without giving away my equally daily vision of their kidnappings and subsequent—I can't bear even to say it. I have housed dogs, answered the door to strangers, driven my car on the highway, after dark, and in strange cities. I have deep-fried things at 385 degrees Fahrenheit, taken showers with the downstairs doors unlocked, eaten a world of foods that could be contaminated, tainted, or harboring botulism. I have had sex and given birth. I have climbed ladders, trees, and cliffs, but never once have I done any of these things or countless others without imagining at least half a dozen horrifying scenarios, like forks in the road that are as easy to turn into as the safe path I almost always have taken. Fear has been my shameful secret and, like most people with shameful secrets, I've felt compelled to trot it out on occasion and make light of it, just to test its power, just to see if it's socially acceptable.

The most grandiose fears I ever had were in 1973 and 1980. In 1973, I spent a week visiting a friend at the L'Abri Fellowship near Lausanne, Switzerland. L'Abri was (and may still be) an intellectual fundamentalist sect, an offshoot of Presbyterianism founded by Dr. Francis Schaeffer. The scenery was spectacular, the food was excellent, and the conversation was stimulating. All the members were well educated, and activities were modeled on those of an exclusive academic conference, with workshops in the morning and lectures at night. I happened to be reading Robert Graves' *The White Goddess* at the time, a good exercise in comparative religion, and my companion was a committed Marxist. These two factors, plus my inborn skepticism, kept me outside the house of Dr. Schaeffer's faith, but did not prevent me from pondering what I heard in the lectures. One of these, by a personable man with lots of literary and art history at his fingertips, was about death. In cool but concrete tones, he spent an hour convincing the audience that we were going to die, each of us, individually and inescapably. Mortal, mortal, mortal. Then, in the last five minutes, and to the considerable relief of everyone in the audience, he offered heaven—eternal life. Ah. Everyone sat back, in possession of the bonus. Except me. I couldn't buy it. I was, however, viscerally convinced that I was going to die. After we left L'Abri, I became progressively more filled with dread, until by the fall, when I was living in a small farmhouse near Iowa City, I was too fearful even to answer the door, even to go looking for the puppy when he got away. At night, I lay awake trying to hear the men I was certain were outside the house, pouring gasoline around the foundation preliminary to setting us alight. I had no faith in my husband's ability to save us, though he was six feet nine inches and athletic. In the spring I learned something about fear: Sometimes it goes away if you do the most

unexpected thing. For me the most unexpected thing was to leave my husband for another man who happened to ride a very large motorcycle and was fearless enough to bend down, at seventy miles per hour, and light his cigarette on the cylinder casing. Action, if it was passionate enough, seemed to beat back fear while courting danger. It worked until I had children.

By 1981, the passionate years were behind me. I owned my own house, car, washing machine, food processor. My daughter was three years old, and after living a life of self-confident adventure for eight whole years, I felt the fear come back, this time of nuclear war. The hostage-taking in Iran may have had something to do with it. (At L'Abri, they were convinced that Iran would be the catalyst for the Final Battle between Christendom and the anti-Christ. Why else, they would ask, would the Soviets have built giant superhighways that ended at the Iranian border?) No doubt the Reaganite drumbeat of anti-Communist propaganda played a role, too. For whatever reasons, I could not leave my daughter at daycare without wondering whether I could get to her in case of missile attack. I couldn't even look out the window of her bedroom, which faced south, without wondering whether we would see the mushroom cloud over Des Moines (a likelier target than Ames, I thought). I tried not to modify my daily routine to accommodate my fears, but it was difficult. Since nuclear war was something I planned for day and night, I decided to write about it, so I wrote a story called "The Blinding Light of the Mind," a difficult story to write because I couldn't figure out how to resolve the situation the narrator found himself in. Then I found out something else about fear—once I had resolved the narrator's situation well enough to end the story and publish it, my fears of nuclear war had dissipated. I was on to only occasionally imagining a runaway vehicle crashing through the line of daycare children as they crossed at the light between the library and the post office. It was disturbing, but it wasn't an obsession.

Palliative though it was, writing wasn't nearly as efficacious as acting out had been. I figured out how to get from day to day, but not how to live without the constant whirring of the inner fear machine as it generated a dreadful parallel life to the actual life I was leading. Other parents I knew talked about their fears, too, so I finally decided that this was the cost of parenthood. It added up to maybe a couple of hours every twenty-four, mostly in the middle of the night, given over to fruitlessness and sweaty sheets.·

Life-taking fear descended again just when I should have predicted it, at the birth of my third child when I was forty-three. There were no complications. The infant was healthy and immediately thriving. No matter. Suffocation. SIDS. Unknowing transmission of the AIDS virus. Sudden madness on the part of one of our dogs. DPT vaccination. My husband rolling over in bed. Stray window-shade cords. Pesticides in my breast milk. Insanity or viciousness in a baby-sitter. My death, which took on new importance as my son's deprivation of his mother. I was writhing underneath an ever weightier load of fear that I could not help adding to with every circumstance that I let myself imagine. The former annoying whir of the fear machine was now more like the roar of a garden chipper in which all my enjoyments and

all my peace of mind were being chewed up.

Then, after twenty years, I resumed horseback riding. The moment was Proustian—I walked into a stable and smelled the sweet, sour, green, moist richness of muck and it filled me with longing. I signed up for lessons. Within two weeks and four lessons, I bought an emaciated gray Thoroughbred with a sweet disposition and excellent manners (later, in true Black Beauty fashion, he turned out to be, I kid you not, an international stakes race winner fallen on hard times). My body remembered some of its old equestrian skills, and after a few weeks my trainer suggested we try jumping. He set up a tiny cross pole. At the sight of it, all my talent for fear manifested itself, this time in my body rather than in my mind. My mouth dried up, my hands began to sweat, all my sinews weakened. I trotted the horse toward the pole, keeping my eyes resolutely on the roof-peak of the barn. He popped over it. My trainer said, "Very good!" and raised the fence to a small vertical—a pole set between two standards, with a ground pole to show the horse the base of the jump. I had the horse trot over that one. My certainty that I was going to fall off and be killed, leaving my children motherless and without an income, was absolute. I didn't know how it was going to happen, but I knew that it was going to. The interesting thing about my fear was that I was feeling it purely rather than making pictures. I was not imagining the actual stages of the disaster, as I generally did, only the appalling result. It was not horror, but terror.

Nothing else about the horse or riding him scared me. Most people who work around horses have been injured at one time or another. A horse is a dangerous animal, more so than a dog or a cat, not only because of its size, but also because of its nature. His instinct is to flee danger at any cost, and to perceive danger in anything strange. As a herd animal, he looks to companions for confirmation of his take on any situation. If others seem afraid, be they horses or people, he takes this as license to react out of fear. If others seem unafraid, he will tentatively control his panic unless circumstances overwhelm him. A panicked horse is an extremely perilous business, flailing, kicking, throwing himself around, sometimes striking or biting or rearing until he flips over backwards. The United States Pony Club advises its members to wear protective headgear whenever they are in the presence of a horse, riding or not. As a result of this policy, horse-related head injuries and deaths have dropped significantly over the last five years. See? I can recite all of these facts, and yet I was unafraid of my new acquisition, pet, obsession, companion animal, dependent. I didn't mind if he bucked or got a little out of hand at the canter. If he lifted his hind leg in a threatening way while I was grooming him, I smacked him and told him to put it down. I soon fancied that he recognized me, and as he fattened, I began to think that he liked me, understood the change in his situation.

But I could not jump, or even think of jumping, without paralyzing fear, even though jumping is the most fun you can have on a horse.

Over the months of daily riding, my fear did not diminish, or even evolve. I took lessons, I practiced, I read books and talked to riders. I even entered competitions. The prospect of the competition always excited me. The reality of the competition, before my turn ever came

to ride, exhausted me. When my turn did come, I felt too tired to drive my horse forward. My legs stuck to his sides, immobile. I was panting. I thought falling off might be a relief because at least I could lie there. I hardly had the strength to steer. Fear was supposed to be invigorating, an adrenaline rush. But before I had ridden more than five minutes, I was ready to get off and, it felt like, take a nap. Of course, this was embarrassing, but fear of failure has never loomed large in my pantheon.

My friend Mary, whose horse has broken her shoulder twice and who wears back and wrist supports in order to ride, is more afraid to play golf than gallop her horse over a stiff cross-country course, because she doesn't want other golfers to see her make a bad shot. Dorothy Trapp, who rides for the United States Equestrian team, of whom other riders say, "Whenever I come to a big fence, I just envision myself riding with my feet on the dashboard, like Dorothy," used to overcome her jitters by reminding herself that no one was expecting her to succeed, or even asking her to try. But others' expectations didn't figure in my fears, and neither did my own. Mine were low and getting lower.

Unfortunately, so were those of my horse.

It is a rare horse who barrels along, calmly and confidently jumping the jumps no matter what the rider is doing or thinking. Some show hunters look like that's what they are doing, but what is really happening is that their trainers are regularly tuning them up so that their riders can ride them. I loved my horse and was proud of him, and from the beginning of our acquaintance, I didn't want our relationship to be diluted by the expertise of another rider. But he soon came to manifest all the signs of waning confidence. Often he refused to jump even small fences, even poles lying on the ground. If he felt the least doubt about a fence—the sun might be reflecting off a panel in an odd way, he might not have seen flowers in front of this fence before—he would act on his doubt and stop to look at it and snort. Other times, he would show doubt by racing at his fences, galloping through them, as if the only way he could sustain the commitment to jump was by going so fast that he couldn't stop. His jumping form was often bad—no bascule, no judgment of the takeoff point, knocking poles down. Over a whole course, errors and panic would compound until at last he refused because he simply didn't know what he was doing. One difference between a horse and a motorcycle is that the horse desires to stay upright, so when my horse felt at risk, he chose not to participate. It was clear to me, though my trainers didn't actually say so (limiting their remarks to instruction rather than diagnosis) that he was taking my fears seriously, perfectly acting out my ambivalence. And devolving further and further in his training. My fault. I realized I had to either stop jumping or learn how, and really learning how meant retrieving some of my own inner space from the fear and exhaustion quartered there.

What I had to learn how to do was the very thing that I couldn't bear, which is to let the horse go forward. A woman I met told me a story. Her daughter was riding a mare that the family had bred and trained over a large intermediate cross-country course (fences about three feet nine inches, up-and-down terrain, tricky approaches). The girl had already suffered a fall and a refusal, so no ribbons were at stake and the girl had begun to ride, in the mother's words, "defensively, backwards." The pair came to a telephone pole swinging over a wide, deep ditch. As with all cross-country fences, the pole was solid—the immovable object. Obedience overcoming caution, the horse tried to jump in spite of the fact that she was traveling too slowly. In the middle of the jump, both horse and rider had the time to look down into the ditch. Both startled. The mare, just rising to the apex of the jump, caught her feet on the pole and flipped, tossing the rider twenty feet and landing upside down in the bottom of the ditch. She lay there, stunned, while the girl ran over, climbed down, and began crying that she had killed the horse. The lucky thing was that she hadn't—the mare came up, leapt to her feet, and scrambled out, unharmed—but every witness knew that death had been a possibility. Even so, the adult human body knows all sorts of reasons against letting the horse go forward. For one thing the horse might get out of control. For another, it's harder for the rider to stay with the horse's center of gravity if it is plunging forward. And the rider has to accept the surge of power that seems to come right up out of the ground through the horse's hocks, haunches, and into the rider's own body. Resistance to that power might mean the rider would rebound from it right off the horse, and yet passivity and limpness might cause the rider to slip off. The rider has to receive, contain, and use the horse's energy. That takes an act of will as well as of coordination. My horse, it was clear, had substituted the wish to run through the jump and get it over with for the desire to go forward, just as I had. I knew that he was less safe without confidence than he had been with confidence, but I didn't really BELIEVE it.

I saw in pictures of me jumping my horse that I looked awkward and incorrect, not to mention unbeautiful. I also saw how low the jumps were. We were barely leaving the ground, and yet together my horse and I had made a very big deal out of the whole endeavor. I think what I saw, after a long life of fear, was just how unattractive fear was. I could say that it compromised the very reasons that I'd resumed riding, both athletic and esthetic, but let's just say it was ugly, made me ugly, made my horse ugly.

I began making him go forward, kicking his sides starting about five strides out from the jump until the takeoff, to make sure that above all things he felt convinced that he must go over the jump. That day, I sensed clearly that he was surprised and, when put to the test, willing enough. He stopped refusing except as an occasional test of my determination. After a few weeks, I could stop kicking him, start expressing my desire to jump more subtly. The reward was that he started going forward more eagerly on his own. When we approached, he would find the place where he wanted to take firm contact with the bit and move toward the jump, needing me not only to go along, but to go along wholeheartedly. Where he once had looked to me for a signal about whether he had to jump almost every jump, now I only had to urge him strongly at the strangest or the largest fences. And if I showed conviction, he jumped them calmly, even eagerly. And yet he wasn't racing at the fences. The power I felt from him was a large-strided, round power, not a quick-strided, flat power. He had the confidence to find his takeoff spot and use his body. He reassumed his former identity as a "good" jumper rather than an awkward one. He got happier.

Of course I would like to say that I now fear nothing, that I no longer knock on wood or mutter "kina hora" under my breath. But there is a real change in my state of mind. There were times after my son was born when it felt like all of my energy and effort might not carry us into the next hour, even the next minute. We ate dinner every Sunday night with some friends who had a three-year-old and a five-year-old. The survival of those children from week to week was unremarkable, expected, but the survival of my own healthy son seemed astounding. It was as if life's momentum had ceased to exist and we had to apply all our intentions to simply continuing in the teeth of the accidents that might happen. These days, though, the fear machine is hardly buzzing, even when I send the children to school, even when I get on an airplane, even when I get into the car. I can only attribute this to going through the physical motions and reaping the physical rewards of overcoming my terror of jumping my horse.

Now, of course, the jumps get higher. There are unknown refinements on the experience of going forward that will have to be learned, but, barring nuclear war, I think we can learn them, *kina hora*.

FRITZ SCHOLDER

dream horses

Devil Horse (1990, bronze)

Dream Horse (1987, acrylic on canvas)

Dream Horse, Leaving (1987, acrylic on paper)

Dream Horse, Leaving #2 (1987, acrylic on paper)

Dream Horse Portrait (1986, acrylic on paper)

Another Dream Horse (1986, bronze)

loving the older horSe

JO-ANN MAPSON

My life was in one of those long, slow skids where you grasp the wheel and try to remember what they taught you in Driver's Ed: turn *into* the skid, not away from it. My marriage was only part of it. I felt failure weighing on my shoulders like a yoke, and I possessed enough rejection slips to paper the walls of my house. My writing was going so badly I couldn't lift my spirits, let alone a pen. I was cleaning houses for a living, but my inner house was a mess. Riding lessons were more affordable than seeing a therapist. Then the worst thing imaginable happened: My trainer was breaking up the riding school and moving north. She offered me Tonto, her oldest lesson horse, a barn-sour Leopard Appaloosa whose back end looked like the losing side of a mud fight. A California girl, I knew enough Spanish to consider the source of his name. *Stupid* had to come from somewhere. The price was $150, which included two Western saddles. Nobody else wanted him. If I didn't take him, he'd go to auction, which translated to the dog food factory. At the time, I believed I needed a different kind of horse, maybe a shiny black thoroughbred overflowing with spirit. But my trainer knew what she was doing matching a sorrowful writer to the crankiest horse in the barn.

Of course, to afford a horse meant I had to clean more houses. It's pretty defeating to clean a thousand toilets, to peer into the porcelain day after day, to strive to make everything that is somebody else's shine. But scrubbing a toilet is nothing compared to a horse whose soul has been bruised to the bone by thousands of strangers miscuing him to halt when they mean walk, to jump the fence when they are clawing painfully on the reins. After many years of such treatment, Tonto was all red flags and bad attitude. My first act as his owner was to take him off the lesson string. Initially, I think he believed he was on vacation. When the endless routine did not resume, I imagined his thoughts went something like this: *Is all this business with the carrots and the soft brushes my last supper? Who in God's name is this woman with the terrible singing voice and why does she persist in aiming these songs at me?*

Slowly, Tonto made the transition into becoming a family horse. He tolerated having his picture taken in cardboard antlers for the Christmas card. He taught my then-young son to appreciate the easy love peculiar to the animal world. Jack often came home from the stables so covered in dirt that I had to take a hose to him in the driveway before I could let him inside the house. From Tonto's back, my son enjoyed the last long Indian summer of his childhood.

This patient animal listened faithfully to my rendition of *South Pacific* deep in the private confines of the Cleveland National Forest. He must have enjoyed the concert, as he often flicked his ears interestedly as I reached for the higher notes, something Mary Martin achieved with ease and I just managed by the grace of my fingernails. Once he spooked at two deer and took me for a long gallop down a fire trail where the notion came to me that reins were indeed illusory. As I pictured my demise, I was forced to discern between terror and exhilaration and realized that the latter had been so absent from my life I was more in danger of dying from security than from this wild ride. When he finally ran out of gas it occurred to me that perhaps he had needed the blast as much as his rider.

Over time, he learned that the arrival of the silver pick-up truck meant cube sugar, molasses-coated oats, and hours of soft, gentle grooming. His demeanor changed from suspicious to interested. A sparkle entered his eye. He nickered when I approached the stall, even without goodies. I found a different job, one where I didn't have to scrub toilets. Every spare moment was spent in this animal's presence, where I was content to bop along with no definite goals. I thought about going back to school, but considered that maybe the happiness I felt now was enough to sustain me. Marriage possesses its inherent ups and downs, and eventually things started to swing up in that area. As for writing, who needed more rejection slips, anyway?

Then my horse decided it was time to teach me his wisdom. At first, I didn't have a clue what was happening. I'd given up on the blank page; I was determined to master fences. Each time I got bucked off, I realized he was only doing what logic and my legs told him to do. We jumped fences, or rather *he* jumped fences, and sometimes I flew and was with him and sometimes I got flung down in the dirt where I belonged. But oh, there were moments when we were more intimate than lovers, each working in concert to achieve lift and purpose, breathless inside that moment of suspension when we became airborne, united, one.

That book that made the bestseller lists, the one about the man who talked to horses? It's bullshit. *Horses talk to people, but only certain people have the right kind of ears to listen back.* I developed a sense of true hearing only after miles of trail riding, after choking down mouthfuls of dirt as I tumbled off his back and, despite my aching bones, climbed back on. *You already know how to write a novel,* Tonto whispered to me. *First, master the basics: saddle, bridle, cues, and for God's sake, don't forget the sugar. Now plot your approach, and please, let's go somewhere new every once in a while. Take your time, we're in no hurry. But bear in mind that eventually it comes down to this: You must approach the fence believing that what is beneath you will sustain you, and meld your center of gravity with what it is you are trying to say. You'll fly or you'll fall, there are no guarantees.*

Maybe all my stories come from this horse, who is now in his thirty-third year, and still explodes into hourlong fits of bucking when it rains. Arthritis has settled into his rear end. There are days he is as forgetful as my grandmother, who died of Alzheimer's. I look at him and sometimes feel I am in possession of this classic old truck with a disintegrating engine, and nobody makes these parts anymore. People suggest to me that I "get rid of him." But when he isn't lame, he gives walk-trot lessons to tiny tots. Kids adore the ugly old grandpa horse. He is the first one they will fall in love with, and when they move on to the thoroughbreds he's okay with that, because he understands his place in the world. In horse vernacular, he is known as "bombproof," incredibly, perfectly safe. These days I'm content to proceed at a walk. There have been times on the trail when I have distractedly nudged him to move on, only to look down and see that he was avoiding a rattlesnake. And then there is the underlying question of relationship, of commitment. Does one have to say "I do" to another like species, one who stands on hind legs, to remain faithful? Seems like a pretty ridiculous question to pose about the horse who saved my life.

Did I save his?

Technically, I suppose plunking down $150 I couldn't afford accomplished that. But it turned out to be so much more than spending money in hopes of healing each other, though we did that, too. Horse ownership delivered me into another realm, where moments like this visit me like pure grace: When I circle my arms around his massive, swan-shaped neck and bury my face in his silver coat, breathing in gulps of his unmistakable heavenly smell, I can't imagine my life without his alongside it.

Last spring, I walked him all night as he colicked. The hours passed, and his condition did not improve. There came a moment when I buried my face in his lathered neck and told him to go if he needed to, that the only pain I could not bear was his. But the next morning, he was still alive, the oldest horse in the stables, not quite yet ready to check out.

Guinness Book of World Records aside, I know that someday soon he will die, and that there are lessons for me in that experience as well. I will consider it an honor to stay by his side and hold a hoof. Then my heart will buck for years and it will likely rain for decades. After the sky has cleared, there will be room for another horse who will have other lessons to teach me. That is how it is with horse people. That is how it will always be for me. Horses, always, coming and going, hoofprints across my heart.

ERIC ROHMANN

taking flight

contributors' notes

DIANE ACKERMAN is a poet and essayist, whose work is continually engaged by the riches of the natural world. Her book *A Natural History of the Senses* was made into a television series for PBS. Her other books include *The Moon by Whale Light*, *A Natural History of Love*, and, most recently, *A Slender Thread*, reflections on her work at a crisis center.

JONIS AGEE, born in Nebraska, reared in Missouri, and longtime resident of Minnesota, has spent a lifetime living with and writing about horses. The author of three collections of stories, *Pretend We've Never Met*, *Bend This Heart*, and *A .38 Special and a Broken Heart*, and three novels, *Sweet Eyes, Strange Angels, and South of Resurrection*, she currently teaches in the MFA program at University of Michigan.

CANDYCE BARNES is the author of several short stories that have appeared in such journals as *The Southern Review* and *Story* and has recently completed her second novel. She does not own that horse farm in Kentucky she always wanted, but resides in Westerville, Ohio, with her husband, Bob, and two Old English sheepdogs, Boots and Todd—horse surrogates.

JANET BIGGS exhibits her installations in museums and galleries in the United States and abroad. She is represented by the Anna Kustera Gallery, and makes her home on New York City's Lower East Side.

RITA MAE BROWN's horse, Peggy Sue, has her first dictated story in this collection. (Sneaky Pie, her cat, has an entire series of mysteries to her credit.) Rita Mae has authored many acclaimed books on her own, including *Riding Shotgun*, a tale of woman who rides through a time warp while fox hunting in Virginia. Other books include the classic *Ruby Fruit Jungle*; *Starting from Scratch*, a writer's manual; and the novels *Venus Envy* and *Southern Discomfort*.

DEBORAH BUTTERFIELD has been creating sculptures of horses from materials that have included barbed wire, fencing, the remains of an airstream trailer, mud, and sticks, as well as more traditional casting and sculptural materials, since the early 1970s. Unlike the militaristic horses of western art history, her creations are often mares, unridden and solitary. Her work has been exhibited and awarded extensively, and is housed in the permanent collections of many of the country's premier institutions, including the Metropolitan Museum of Art, Hirshhorn Museum, Walker Art Center, and the Art Institute of Chicago. She lives and works on a ranch in Montana.

PATRICIA CRONIN is an artist whose first solo show, "Pony Tales," was exhibited at Wooster Gardens, New York City, in January 1997. Her paintings have been reviewed in *The New York Times, Art Forum, Art in America, Los Angeles Times* and *OUT*. She lives in New York City, where she is fortunate to live an urban life *and* ride at Claremont Riding Academy near Central Park and Kensington Stables in Prospect Park in Brooklyn.

JOHN DERRYBERRY, based in Dallas, photographs across the nation for his commissioned portrait work. Currently he's preparing a book and exhibition project concerning Australian Aboriginal body painting for the Sydney Olympics in 2000.

TODD DEVRIESE is an artist and teacher who has been involved in printmaking for more than fifteen years, showing at such places as The Lowe Gallery, Atlanta, and the University of Wisconsin-Milwaukee Art Museum. He holds fine arts degrees from Illinois and Ohio State universities. He is director of the Ohio State Fair Fine Arts Exhibition and a faculty member of the Ohio State University's regional campus in Marion, Ohio.

GRETEL EHRLICH travels extensively for her writing, often on assignment for magazines such as *Time, Harper's, Atlantic Monthly,* and *Architectural Digest*. Her books include *Questions of Heaven: The Chinese Journeys of an American Buddhist, The Solace of Open Spaces,* and *A Match to the Heart*. She lives on a ranch in California.

BART FORBES, an artist and illustrator, often works in the sporting fields, and has created theme paintings and posters for a variety of PGA and Seniors tournaments, the Boston Marathon, New York Marathon, Americas Cup, and Indianapolis 500. He has also designed over 20 commemorative postage stamps for the U. S. Postal Service. As official artist for the Seoul Olympics, his paintings of the events are currently housed in the Olympic Museum in Seoul.

TESS GALLAGHER's most recent books of poetry are *Portable Kisses, Moon Crossing Bridge*, and, in Great Britain, *My Black Horse: New and Selected Poems*. She is also the author of two books of short stories, *The Lover of Horses* and *At the Owl Woman Saloon*, as well as a book of essays, *A Concert of Tenses*. She has been guest faculty at a number of distinguished universities, and lives in Washington state.

GARY GILDNER has published fifteen books, which include collections of poetry—most recently *The Bunker in the Parsley Fields*, recipient of the Iowa Poetry Prize—short stories, a novel, and a memoir entitled *The Warsaw Sparks*, about coaching a baseball team in Communist Poland. He currently lives on a ranch in Idaho's Clearwater Mountains.

LUCY GREALY is the author of the memoir *Autobiography of a Face*, published in 1994, as well as a poet and essayist. Her work appears widely in journals and magazines.

JOY HARJO, an enrolled member of the Muscogee Nation, currently resides in Albuquerque, New Mexico. She has published many books of poetry, including *She Had Some Horses*. She recently co-edited an anthology of native women's writing, *Reinventing the Enemy's Language*. Harjo also plays saxophone and performs her poetry with her band, Poetic Justice, which has traveled internationally; their recent compact disc is "Letter from the End of the Twentieth Century."

JANA HARRIS is a poet, novelist, short story writer, and essayist living in the foothills of the Cascade Mountains, where she and her husband raise horses. Her books include *Manhattan as a Second Language, Oh How Can I Keep on Singing?, Alaska,* and a book-length epic poem, *The Dust of Everyday Life*. She teaches creative writing at the University of Washington.

SHELBY HEARON is the acclaimed author of fourteen novels, including *Footprints, Life Estates*, and *Owning Jolene*. A longtime resident of Texas and New York, she currently lives in Burlington, Vermont, where she is visiting professor at Middlebury College.

IVARS HEINRIHSONS, professor of Fine Arts at the Latvian Academy of Art, has participated in more than a hundred solo and group exhibitions throughout the world during the last twenty years.

JANE HIRSHFIELD's poetry has been collected in four volumes; the most recent one is *The Lives of the Heart*. She has also edited and co-translated two collections by female poets from the past, and is the author of a book of essays, *Nine Gates: Entering the Mind of Poetry*. Her work appears in periodicals such as *The New Yorker, The Atlantic Monthly, The New Republic, and The Nation*. She currently lives in the San Francisco Bay Area.

MICHAEL HOUGHTON has been a photographer for more than twenty-five years, working primarily in Ohio. His pictures often appear in architectural and interior trade magazines, but his great passion is photographing the West.

PAM HOUSTON's first collection of stories, *Cowboys Are My Weakness*, won her immediate attention. Since then, she has taught in the MFA writing programs of several universities and has written articles for various magazines, including *Condé Nast Sports for Women*, where she is a contributing editor. Her latest book of fiction is *Waltzing the Cat*.

MICHELLE HUNEVEN was the sometimes proud and usually baffled owner of two great cow ponies, Ramon and Whitey, and a very tiny Welsh-Shetland pony cross, appropriately named Raisin. She survives them all, albeit with damaged vertebrae and the occasional evocative muscle spasm, in Los Angeles, where she makes her living as a restaurant critic and freelance writer. Her first novel, *Round Rock,* was published in 1997.

MAXINE KUMIN, winner of the 1973 Pulitzer Prize in Poetry, has published twelve collections of poems, four novels, several children's books, and three books of essays, many of which concern horses. She is a chancellor of the Academy of American Poets and lives with her husband on a farm in New Hampshire.

ROBB KENDRICK has traveled in the past several years to fifty-four countries and all seven continents on photographic assignments ranging from the Sherpas of the Himalayas to the state of global fishing. He works half a year for *National Geographic* and the other half shooting advertising campaigns and corporate projects, and for publications such as *Life, Audubon, Sports Illustrated, and Smithsonian*. A native of Spur, Texas, he currently lives near Austin.

SUE KYLLÖNEN has been a portrait photographer for many years, with much of her focus on the quality of life experienced by her subjects, including senior citizens for social service agencies and people living with AIDS and HIV. She has a lifelong passion and commitment to riding and and to horses as both individuals and athletes.

FRANZ LIDZ is a truly unorthodox spirit. A senior writer at *Sports Illustrated* who had covered only one sporting event— a pigeon race—before joining the magazine in 1980, he lives with an assortment of animals (turkey, cats, Great Pyrenees, llamas, and chickens, which are all named after cheeses) on his six-acre spread, Barmy Farm. A commentator for NPR and a monthly columnist for MicroSoft's online adventure/travel magazine, his oeuvre covers everything from black-fly biting festivals to the British lawn-mowing championships. The film *Unstrung Heroes* is based on his book of the same name.

JO-ANN MAPSON's novels—*Hank & Chloe, Blue Rodeo, and Saddle Ranch*—explore the changing West. In 1996, *Blue Rodeo* was produced as an original CBS movie. Mapson is also the author of a short story collection entitled *Fault Line*. Her family descends from turn-of-the-century lemon growers and tobacco farmers, and is active in all phases of the horse industry from show-jumping to barrel-racing to English equitation.

CLEOPATRA MATHIS's most recent book of poems is *Guardian*. She teaches English and creative writing at Dartmouth College in Hanover, New Hampshire.

T. M. MCNALLY's short stories have appeared in the *Gettysburg Review, Hudson Review, Iowa Review, Ploughshares, Southern Review, Yale Review, and the O'Henry Prize Anthology*. He is the author of a collection of short stories entitled *Low Flying Aircraft* and a novel, *Almost Home*. He lives in St. Louis.

MEREDITH MONK is a composer, singer, filmmaker, choreographer, and director. A pioneer in extended vocal technique and interdisciplinary performance, she has created more than a hundred works spanning a career of thirty years, including "Book of Days," aired on PBS, "Volcano Songs," "Dolmen Music," and *Atlas: An Opera in Three Parts*, which features her fascination with horses. Among her awards and citations are three Obies—one for Sustained Creative Achievement—two Guggenheim fellowships, and sixteen ASCAP Awards for Musical Composition.

MICHAEL PARASKEVAS is a fine arts painter and illustrator. With his mother, Betty Paraskevas, he has published several children's books, including the Junior Kroll series. A number of their works are being adapted for television and film. Paraskevas lives on Long Island and often paints the equestrian environment.

MICHAEL PLANK, a painter and illustrator, creates works for magazines, children's books, and greeting cards, as well as the gallery. He lives in Shawnee, Kansas.

THOMAS RABBITT is the author of several collections of poetry. His first, *Exile*, won the Pitt Prize. His most recent, *The Transfiguration of the Dead*, is an illustrated fine arts edition. After twenty-six years in Alabama, he has returned to Cape Cod. He still has two Arabian mares.

ERIC ROHMANN is a printmaker, painter, and children's book author, whose recent books include *Time Flies* (which won a Caldecott Honor), *The Cinder-Eyed Cats*, and *King Crow*. His work has been exhibited and collected throughout the United States.

DAVID ROMTVEDT is a composer and musician in a Carribean-basin band, The Fire Ants, whose first compact disc was released in 1997. As a writer, his body of work includes short stories, personal essays, and several volumes of acclaimed poetry. His most recent collection, *Windmill: Essays from Four Mile Ranch*, contains stories from the farm he works in Wyoming.

FRITZ SCHOLDER is a painter, sculptor, and printmaker of international renown and a recipient of numerous awards in the last thirty years including fellowships from the Whitney, Rockefeller, and Ford foundations. In 1991 he received the Norsk Hostfest Humanitarian Award, and in 1996 he received the Visionary Award from the Institute of American Indian Arts; he also is a past honoree and present patron of the American Academy of Achievement. The subject of eleven books and three PBS documentaries, Scholder has exhibited work in museums throughout the world, most recentl, in Japan, China, France, Germany, and at the Hermitage Museum in St. Petersburg, Russia.

ROBIN SCHWARTZ's photographs are widely exhibited and published, and are held in the permanent collections of institutions including the Metropolitan Museum of Art, the Museum of Modern Art, and the Bibliothèque Nationale in Paris. Her first two books, *Like Us: Primate Portraits* and *Dog Watching*, explored the predicament of our fascination with animals. Her current work is focused on children and animals in Mexico.

DEBBIE SHARP fled Los Angeles after a fifteen-year career in the high-power high-stress side of the film business to regain her own creativity as an independent filmmaker and screenwriter. She currently lives in New York and has just completed her first project, "Sparky Moves to Manhattan."

JANE SMILEY won the Pulitzer Prize for her novel, *A Thousand Acres*, which was made into a film in 1997. Her other books include *Moo* and *The Age of Grief*, nominated for a National Book Critics Award. She lives in California.

LINDY SMITH, who grew up in Iowa, holds degrees in photography and French from Bennington College and l'Université de Caen. Following a twenty-year hiatus, she returned to photography—and started riding—after observing a horsemanship clinic in Wyoming in 1992.

HENRY TAYLOR is a professor of literature and co-director of the graduate program in creative writing at American University, where he has taught since 1971. His four volumes of poetry include *Poetry for the Flying Change*, winner of the 1986 Pulitzer Prize, and *Understanding Fictions: Poems, 1986-1996*.

JAMIE WYETH is the third generation of a dynasty of American painters that includes his grandfather N. C. Wyeth and his father, Andrew Wyeth. Jamie is a sensitive observer of his rural surroundings, depicting livestock and other beasts with the same care and intensity he devotes to his portraits of people. In 1998, The Farnsworth Center for the Wyeth Family in Maine, a new study center devoted to the Wyeth family's art, opened in an historic church property on the museum's campus.

PAUL ZARZYSKI has been writing poetry for nearly twenty-five years. During twelve of those years, he also rode bareback broncs on both amateur and professional rodeo circuits. One of the most celebrated "cowboy poets," he has toured internationally, recorded and read his work extensively, and published several chapbooks and two full collections of poetry.

Michael J. Rosen began The Company of Animals Fund in 1990 with the generosity of twenty-two short story writers and revenues from the anthology that included their works. Six other books have followed, commissioning more than 200 other writers, illustrators, photographers, and children's book authors to donate their talents toward animal welfare efforts. At this writing, the Fund has offered offered direct service grants to more than sixty-five shelters and humane societies around the country, with funds exceeding $275,000. Primarily, grants have sponsored some form of veterinary care, most often to families otherwise unable to afford or provide the necessary treatment. With this book, funds are designed for a variety of equine rescue efforts. For more information about the Fund, please write to the editor in care of Artisan, 708 Broadway, New York, New York 10003.

credits and acknowledgments

The editor would, once again, like to express his thanks to Jennifer McNally and the other guiding voices behind The Company of Animals Fund. Thanks, too, to Evan Fisher and Will Shively for their assistance with this book. My boundless gratitude, as ever, to Mark Svede.

Page 11, "Astride the Twilight," copyright © 1998 Diane Ackerman; pages 12-15, "My Grandfather and His Belgians," copyright © 1998 Gary Gildner; pages 16-18, "Boots, Saddle, To Horse, and Away!," copyright © 1998 Candyce Barnes; pages 19-23, "Horsey Girl," photographs copyright © 1998 Janet Biggs; pages 24-25, "Horse Riffs (A Journal)," copyright © 1998 Meredith Monk; pages 2-3 and 26-29, "Jumping," paintings copyright ©1998 Michael Paraskevas; pages 30-33, "Nothing But Trouble Since the Day He Was Born," copyright © 1998 Jana Harris; pages 34-38, "Three Stories," copyright © 1998 David Romtvedt; pages 6-7, 39-41, and endpapers, "Westward," photographs copyright © 1998 Michael Houghton; pages 42-43, "Horsepower," copyright © 1998 Shelby Hearon; page 44, "Wyoming," photograph copyright © 1998 Lindy Smith; pages 45-47, "Side-View: A Mother's Perspective," copyright © 1998 Cleopatra Mathis; pages 48-49, "Connemara," paintings copyright © 1998 Jamie Wyeth; pages 50-52, "Working with Humans," copyright © 1998 Rita Mae Brown; pages 53-56, "Breaking Horses: A Seduction in Letter Form," copyright © 1998 Pam Houston; pages 57-59, "City Horses," illustrations copyright © 1998 Michael Plank; pages 60-63, "Angel Foot: A Double Portrait," copyright © 1998 Tess Gallagher; pages 64-66, "Goldart," copyright © 1998 Henry Taylor, appeared in a different version in *Virginia Quarterly Review*; pages 67-69, A suite of paintings copyright © 1998 Ivars Heinrihsons; "Restraint of the Horse" on page 68 is in The Norton and Nancy Dodge Collection of Nonconformist Art, Jane Voorhees Zimmerli Art Museum, Rutgers, the State University of New Jersey; pages 70-73, "Paperback Rider: An Interview with Dick Francis" copyright © 1998 Franz Lidz; pages 74-77, "The Power of Horses," copyright © 1998 Joy Harjo; pages 78-81, "Obsolete: Not for Navigational Purposes," collages copyright © 1998 Todd DeVriese; pages 82-86, "Summer School," copyright © 1998 T. M. McNally; pages 1 and 87-89, "Horse and Camera," photographs copyright © 1998 Sue Kyllönen; pages 90-93, "On Whitey," copyright © 1998 Michelle Huneven; pages 94-96, "Work Horses," sculptures copyright © 1998 Deborah Butterfield; pages 97-102, "Good Horse Keeping," copyright © 1998 Paul Zarzyski; poems reprinted with permission from *All This Way for the Short Ride: Roughstock Sonnets 1971-1996*, by the Museum of New Mexico Press, copyright © 1996; page 103, "Red Bandanna," painting copyright © 1998 Bart Forbes; pages 104-107, "Horses Cross, Donkeys Cross," copyright © 1998 Jane Hirshfield; pages 108-109, "Kashmir," photographs copyright © 1998 John Derryberry; pages 110-112, "The Bluebird of Happiness," copyright © 1998 Gretel Ehrlich; pages 113-114, "Glory Days," copyright © 1998 Maxine Kumin; pages 115-119, "Sparky Moves to Manhattan," video copyright © 1998 Debbie Sharp; pages 120-125, "Big," copyright © 1998 Jonis Agee; pages 126-129, "The Arabber Series," photographs copyright © 1998 Robin Schwartz; pages 130-133, "Rescue," copyright © 1998 Lucy Grealy; pages 134-135, "Pony Tales," paintings copyright © 1998 Patricia Cronin; pages 136-139, "Impossible Horses," copyright © 1998 Tom Rabbitt; pages 5 and 140-141, "Texas, USA," photographs copyright © 1998 Robb Kendrick; pages 142-148, "Puissance," copyright © 1998 Jane Smiley, originally appeared in *Flyway*, the Spring 1995 publication of Iowa State University; pages 149-151, "Dream Horses," paintings and sculptures copyright © 1998 Fritz Scholder; pages 152-154, "Loving the Older Horse," copyright © 1998 Jo-Ann Mapson; page 155, "Taking Flight," painting copyright © 1998 Eric Rohmann.